D1741018

Hunting The West Memphis Boogeyman

Written By

Amanda Pettrey and David Pietras

Cover design by
Amanda Pettrey and David Pietras

1 2 3 4 5 6 7 8 9 10 14

I dedicate this book to Tabatha Wilburn.

You gave me the ray of sunshine I needed

When all I could see were the clouds

The Victims

Steve Edward Branch, eight-years-old, 4 ft. 2, 65 lbs., blonde hair. Last seen in blue jeans, white t-shirt on a black and red bicycle

Christopher Byers, eight-years-old, 4 ft., 52 lbs., light brown hair. Last seen in blue jeans, dark shoes, and white long sleeve shirt

Michael Moore, eight-years-old, 4 ft. 2, 55 lbs., brown hair. Last seen in blue pants, blue Boy Scouts of America shirt, orange and blue Boy Scout hat on a light green bicycle.

[Sources: Missing person reports, autopsies. The clothes found were slightly different.]

Prologue

On May 5th, 1993, as daylight disappeared, the round moon crested the Memphis skyline. It was a view that so many times accompanied a grizzly horror story. The Mississippi River, at that time turbid and swollen from a season of floods, separated the Tennessee Metropolis from its Arkansas namesake, West Memphis. West Memphis is a small town with major highways crisscrossing its heart, with a trucking hub and home to just over 30,000 people. As evening approached the small town, three eight year old boys had already been missing for two hours. By the next day they would be found dead, brutalized, hog-tied and sunken in a ditch.

Dana Moore, mother of victim Michael Moore, last saw her son from a distance as he and his friends disappeared around a bend. Her son was in his Cub Scout uniform riding his bicycle while his second grade schoolmates, Chris Byers and Stevie Branch shared a bike. Childhood friend, Kim

Williams said that she had accompanied Michael and Stevie to the edge of a patch of woods called Robin Hood Hills. Another childhood friend said Chris Byers dropped by his house. This neighbor said Chris told him his stepfather had whipped him and he was running away from home.

Mark Byers, the stepfather of Chris, was a hefty six foot five. Full-bearded and sporting long hair often tied back in a ponytail, the left side of his face drooped from damage from seizures. Changing into overalls and a long-sleeved shirt he headed out on a frantic eighteen hour search, patrolling the neighborhood with his wife, Melissa and his thirteen year-old stepson, Ryan. He would later complain of receiving virtually no help from the authorities. "I called the Sheriff's Department the second time. I said, look, I've had one police officer out here helping me look for these boys." [Mark Byers, May 19, 1993 interview] Byers would describe two occasions when his search took him to the area where the victim's bodies were found. "I was out looking until 4:30 a.m. I walked within 10 or 15 feet of where the

bodies were found and I didn't see them."
[Mark Byers, quoted in West Memphis
Evening Times, May 7th, 1993]

Terry Hobbs, wiry tough with a thick
frowning mustache and a glassy gaze, was
the stepfather of victim Stevie Branch. He
described beginning his search well before
nightfall, including passing near the
discovery site. Terry would wait until the
evening closing time at his wife's restaurant
to inform her of her son's disappearance. To
some this does not sound like the actions of
a loving and caring step parent. You would
think that the mother of the child missing
would be the first person you contact. But
this is only the beginning of the questions
that surround Terry Hobbs.

Recently, Hobbs' companion during his
search has contradicted his account and
DNA and other evidence have been
suggestive of his involvement in the
murders.

Hobbs had made a statement in court in
2009 that he had not seen his stepson Stevie

at all that day. But a neighbor clearly remembers him in the presence of all 3 victims around 6:30 pm on the day that they were reported missing. The neighbor was never questioned by the police, even though she only lived a few houses away.

The neighbor stated that all 3 of the boys rode through her yard on bicycles around 6:30 pm on the evening that they came up missing. She said that she came out of her house at 6:30 that evening to go to church. She stated that she yelled at Christopher to go home. He responded with, *"I don't have to do what you tell me to do."* The neighbor also stated that she saw Terry Hobbs coming down the sidewalk towards her house. She said that he was calling for Stevie to come back down to their house. At that time the neighbor said that she got into her vehicle with her family and left for church. She also stated that all three of the boys and Terry Hobbs were together when she drove past them.

The one thing that makes this neighbor a credible witness is the fact that the neighbor personally knew Stevie and Terry. So there is no chance that she accidently misidentified a stranger as Terry Hobbs like you would expect when someone identifies a total stranger.

Unfortunately this is not the only issue in the web that is called a court case regarding these three children. As we weave our way through the maze of this case we will point out evidence that was overlooked by the local police investigators. And we will focus on statements from witnesses and inconsistencies in stories and facts regarding this case.

We will not go as far as to say that any one single person is guilty beyond a reasonable doubt. But what we will provide you are the real facts of this case. And all we ask is that you take these facts and look at them with an open mind and see if you can tell who "The Boogeyman of West Memphis" is.

One of the biggest obstacles that law enforcement had was the fact that this case was being tried in the media. People were coming out of the woodwork screaming about the occult and devil worshipping. Society focused so much on the devil worshipping aspect of the case that the investigation was also going into that direction.

People came forward with eyewitness accounts of what they claim to have seen on that day. The bad part was the fact that most of the leads sent to the West Memphis Police were fabricated. The media made this case into a Salem style witch hunt. They avoided the true facts of the case and focused solely on the rumors and fabrications that could sell their papers or put viewers in front of the TV during the 6 o'clock news.

Most supporters of the West Memphis Three only have the knowledge of the case from what the media put forth. They either don't know about or just want to ignore any evidence that pointed to the three teenagers arrested.

Outside of the fact that it is a known fact that Damien Echols lied about his whereabouts on the day that the three boys were murdered, and credible eye witnesses placed him in the neighborhood of the killings on the day of the crime there is also physical evidence that is so commonly overlooked by the supporters of The West Memphis Three.

But before we go any further let me take this time to say this. The purpose of this book is to show "all" of the evidence of the case. Not to just point fingers at certain people. I want to present to you the reader all of the evidence that shows the possibility of guilt. And as you go further into the story you will see some other suspects and the evidence against them also. My goal is to give you the "truth" and not to put any misleading spins on the information like the media does to sell papers.

I will also like to say that anything that we present here as fact was obtained from the actual police and or court files on this case. There are so many lies that have presented as fact in this case and I think that the people who accept it are not educated enough to take the time to check the statements that they read. If you read something in this book that conflict with what you have been lead to believe then I advise you to search the information to determine the truth.

CHAPTER ONE
MAY 5TH 1993
MISSING IN A SMALL
TOWN

From left to right: Christopher Byers, Michael Moore, and
Steve Branch

According to the police reports filed by the
families of the three boys, they were last
seen together between 5:30 p.m. and 6:00
p.m. on the evening of 5 May 1993. The
three boys had finished school for the day at
Weaver Elementary School at 3:00 p.m.
Steven Branch went home but shortly
afterwards Michael came to the house to ask
if Steven could come out and play and the

two of them left together at 3:30. Before they left, Stevie's mother Pam Hobbs, gave Stevie strict instructions to be back home by 4:30 and told him that if he wasn't, he would be grounded for two weeks from riding his bike.

According to Pam, about 5 minutes later around 3:35, Christopher came over and asked if Stevie was home, she was surprised that he hadn't ran into them outside because they had just left a few minutes before.

Christopher Byers' step-father, John Mark Byers, said that he had arrived home at 3:10 p.m. but Christopher was not there when his brother Ryan arrived home at 3:30 p.m.

John Mark Byers drove Ryan to the courthouse for a 4:00 p.m. appointment. After dropping Ryan off, he then drove to pick up his wife, Melissa Byers from work. They both arrived back at their home at around 5:20 p.m. only to find that Chris was still not at home, even though there was evidence that he had been there. Soon after bringing Melissa home, John Mark Byers had to leave once again to pick up Ryan from the courthouse, but on the way he found Christopher riding a skateboard. John Byers said that he took his son home where he gave him "two or three licks" with a belt, in the presence of his mother Melissa, as punishment for not staying at home as he had been instructed. Before returning to the courthouse to pick up Ryan, Byers told Christopher to clean up the carport area. Byers said that this was about 5:30 and that this was the last time that he had seen Christopher. According to the West Memphis Police, Christopher had left his home and met up with his friends (James) Michael Moore and Steven Branch soon after 5:30 p.m.

At about 6:00 p.m., Diana Moore said that she had seen her son (James) Michael riding bicycles with Steven Branch and Christopher Byers. Chris had been sitting on the back of Steven's bike.

A neighbor living only three doors down from Steven Branch said that she saw all three of the boys come riding through her yard on their bicycles around 6:30 pm that evening as she and her family were getting ready to go to church. She yelled at Christopher telling him that he needed to go on home. He looked back and told her, "*I don't have to do what you tell me to do.*" The neighbor said at that point she saw Steven's step-father, Terry Hobbs, coming down the sidewalk walking toward her house. She said that he was calling for Stevie to come back down to their house. She saw the boys heading in that direction as she got into her vehicle with her family and left to go to church. As their car drove past them, she saw all three of the boys were with Terry Hobbs. She was never questioned by the West Memphis Police after the children went missing and she did not think that this information was significant. Until she later learned that Terry Hobbs had stated in court that he had not seen his stepson Stevie at all that day.

This eyewitness report places Terry Hobbs with Stevie as well as the other two boys on the evening of his disappearance.

Later in the investigation people would question the reason as to why Terry decided not to inform the police that he was with the boys around 6:30 that day.

John Mark Byers claims that he arrived home from the courthouse with Ryan around 6:30 p.m. to find that Chris was again not at home. Melissa was inside on the phone with her boss and had not been aware that Chris was gone. John, Melissa and Ryan Byers left their home just after 6.30 p.m. to drive around the neighborhood in order to find Chris. During the course of this search, Byers informed a police officer of his son's disappearance. Many people question why he was so adamant to start searching for Christopher at 6:30, so soon after Christopher left the house. According to Byers, he was told by an officer to wait until 8:00 p.m. before making an official report with the police. This is common practice with young children that are reported missing. In most instances the child will eventually show back up at home later in the evening. Byers then explained to the officer that the reason he was so concerned was that Chris had never disappeared like this before. This statement was later contradicted by Christopher's mother Melissa Byers, during an interview on 25 May 1993, when she told police that Christopher had disappeared on several other occasions for hours at a time.

Throughout the investigation numerous people came forward to report that they had seen the boys on the day that they came up missing. The latest sighting was at around 7 p.m. when a witness saw them going toward Robin Hood woods.

These are the last known sightings of the three boys reported to the West Memphis Police.

Morning until 2:45pm - at school

2:45pm – Stevie Branch walks home from school with Pam and Amanda

3:00pm - Stevie Branch arrives home

3:00pm-3:15pm (approx.) - Michael Moore arrives at Stevie's on his bike

3:15pm (approx.) - Stevie and Michael leave the house to ride their bikes. Stevie is told to be back by 4:30pm. The boys leave; go west on South McAuley, then north on 14th.

3:35 pm (approx.) - Christopher Byers comes to the home of Stevie Branch. Pam Hobbs tells him that Stevie and Michael just left, so Chris leaves in search of his friends.

4-4:15pm - Gregory Quirt reports seeing Stevie and Michael with a bunch of other boys. He says they told him they were going "riding". Quirt described seeing 3 boys on 2 bikes (unconfirmed as to whether the 3rd boy on the bike was Chris).

5:15pm - (approx.) David Jacoby states that he saw Stevie and two boys pass by outside of his home.

5:00-5:30pm - Jeff Martins/Betty Lou Martins - see 4 boys (3 on two bikes, and 1 walking). They identified Chris, Michael, and Stevie. The approximate distance from the Hobbs' house (near Jacoby's house) and the Martins' house on 719 Wilson is half a mile.

5:45pm - The Baileys report seeing Stevie and Michael on WE Catt, wearing green backpacks, riding bikes. Michael told Otto Bailey that he was in a hurry and needed to leave. The boys are going toward Mayfair.

5:45pm-6:00pm - Kim Williams is seen in the same location as Stevie and Michael until she is called in by her father. Claims she last saw the two boys heading into Robin Hood woods by way of the Goodwin entrance.

6:00pm - Ben Crafton confirms that Kim was with Stevie and Michael until being called in by her father.

5:45 - 5:50 pm. - Debra O'Tinger says the boys meet up in her yard at 1309 Goodwin Avenue

6:00pm - Jason Gobbell reports seeing 2 boys on bikes

6:00pm - Dana Moore saw three boys on two bikes on N 14th.

6-6:30pm - Chris, Michael, and Stevie are seen playing in the Clark's backyard (a few houses down from the Hobbs' house). Jamie Clark Ballard stated that she heard Terry Hobbs call Stevie back to the house.

6-6:30pm - All three boys are seen by Cindy Rico. She said she saw them by "the drainage ditch down past Blue Beacon down by the bridge."

6:45pm - (questionable sighting) Bryan Woody said he saw 4 boys playing on Goodwin (not confirmed as Stevie, Michael, and Chris)

7pm - Chris Wahl says he saw Christopher and Stevie riding bikes. He refers to one boy as a blonde. It was 7 p.m. because Chris Wahl just got out of night school at that time and saw the boys after class let out. The boys were going toward Robin Hood woods. He reported that it was beginning to get dark. He was polygraphed about involvement and did not indicate deception to questions asking if he was involved.

*** NOTE *** All of these sightings are in the vicinity of the Robin Hood woods where the bodies would later be found. Also note that the times that each witness gave could be off by a few minutes as they are just guessing at the time. The only exceptions are Jamie Clark Ballard who was heading to church at the time of the sighting and Chris Wahl as he just got out of night school when he saw the boys. These two witnesses were 100% certain on the time frame of their sightings that Wednesday evening when the three children would be reported missing.

At 8:08 p.m. John Mark Byers called the West Memphis Police Department to report that his step-son Christopher was still missing. West Memphis Police Officer Regina Meek responded to the Byers' home to take the report.

Fifteen minutes later, Diana Moore spoke with John Mark Byers. She told him that she had seen the three boys at 6:00 p.m. Byers said that this was the first time he had been aware that Chris was with Steven and Michael.

Robin Hood Hills
The road at the top of the picture is the entrance to Robin Hood Hills at West McAuley Dr.

John Mark Byers began to search the Robin Hood Hills area with Diana Moore, Melissa Byers and his step-son Ryan Clark. This was the last known location of the boys. According to Byers, it was already dark by then. At some time between 8:30 p.m. and 10:30 p.m., Byers went home alone to change out of the shorts and flip flops that he had been wearing, into a pair of overalls and boots. At the time that he left, the search party consisted of Ryan Clark, Ritchie Masters, Brett Smith and his sister, along with many others. Later that night they were joined by Officer Moore from the West Memphis Police Department, who would continue to search with them from 10:20 until 11:00 p.m.

Mr. Bojangles

The West Memphis police received a call from Marty King, the manager of the Bojangles restaurant located at 1551 N. Missouri, three quarters of a mile directly west along the bayou diversion channel from The Robin Hood Hills at 8:40 pm on the night of the children's disappearance.

The notes from the police log read: "Bojangles - B/M - towards Delta - bleeding - WW/cap - blue shirt - blk. pants - cast R arm" The call went to Officer Regina Meek., the same officer that had taken the report from John Byers that his son, Christopher was missing, only a few minutes before.

As Marty King explained, a black male, muddy, disoriented and bleeding was inside the women's restroom. There was blood and feces on the floor, stall and walls. A toilet paper roll was soaked to the core with blood.

Officer Meek arrived at the Bojangles at 8:50 pm. She didn't enter the restaurant, instead, pulling up to the drive-through window. She was informed there that the bleeding man had already left. Officer Meek spent the next few minutes searching for him outside. At 9:01 pm, she received yet another call. Someone was egging a house. (From later notes, it was one egg.) Officer Meek responded.

After this incident was released to the public, law enforcement officers across the county commented on the actions of officer Meek that night. With a report of a man bleeding, it would be standard operating procedure to investigate the area where the man was seen. (In this case the bathroom stall). At the time of the call it was not known the overall situation of this man. Was he shot, stabbed or did he suffer a life threatening wound? Many people in the law enforcement field say that the actions taken by officer Meeks are totally in conflict with the training of police officers.

The next day, Officer Covington was speaking to the manager of Bojangles and, in light of the discovery of the murdered boys; he requested that this be followed-up. (Covington was off-duty. In fact, he is the only evening shift officer on duty the fifth of May who is not listed for the sixth of May.)

The police notes for the May 6th visit to the Bojangles restaurant are listed here. Note that any typos in the statements were not corrected to keep the integrity of the story in tact:

5/6/93 Received call to go to Bo-Jangles + talk to the Manager.

5/6/93 9:00 P.M. Det. Sgt. Allen + Det. Ridge went to Bo-Jangles + talked with the manager, a Marty King [address and phone redacted]. Marty King related that they had a Black / male on 5/5/93 Between 9:00 - 9:30 PM that a Black / male was found the ladies bathroom bleeding from the arm. the Manager stated that the black man was 5-11, thin dirty, late 20's, pair of sunglasses were left in toilet suspected by Black / male. Subject had a blue cast type brace on his arm that had white Velcro on it. the Black male appeared to be mental / + disorentated (Not intoxicated or under influence of drugs) Police were called Subject left out on foot + Walked East toward the back dumpster then [inserted here: Black males clothing was denim sleeveless shirt, Black shoes, look like tennis shoes. Black thin warm up pants.] came back out to Missouri + walked torward Delta Service Station.

Det. Ridge took blood scrapings from North Wall inside women's bathroom above toliet, took blood scrapings from inside of door to women's bathroom + Entrance hall to bathroom From Sitting Area at Bojangles. [signed] Mike Allen

Bojangles description (summary from police log notes and 5/6 report):

Late 20's.

5'11

Thin

Blue cast with white Velcro on his right arm.

Blue denim sleeveless shirt

Black shoes

Black thin warm up pants.

Disoriented, bleeding.

Marty King described the mystery man in the bathroom as having mud on his pants similar to the way the two officers had mud on their pants -- and this was after the officers had been in the ditch where the bodies of the three murdered children had been found.

Was there a second sighting of the

Bojangles man? During the door to door interviews there was this comment from a neighbor on Wilson:

"Bill H. - saw nothing but said we need to talk to Mrs. C. 735-xxxx. She works for Schneider Truck Lines evening shift. She said a driver saw a man with blood all over him Wed night."

Three trucks from Schneider National visited the Blue Beacon Truck Wash after 7 pm on Wednesday.

The West Memphis police looked at two suspects as possibly being the elusive Mr. Bojangles, although this was six or more weeks after the crime. From police notes (misspellings intact):

6/24/93 Talked with a Larry Ceasar who has been known in the past to of worn a brace on his right arm, from an injury (gunshot wound) to shoulder. Larry Ceaser fits the general description of that given by the

Bojagles manager of a B/M that came into Bojagles on 05/05/93 with the exception that Larry Ceaser has a full beard & is known to this investigator as always wearing a beard. Larry Ceaser was asked about wearing an arm brace during the month of May. Larry Ceaser who has a crippled right arm stated he hadn't worn a arm brace since back around Thanksgiven, this was verified in reference to arm brace by Otis Ceaser, & Robert Ceaser, brother of Larry Ceasers. the radio log on May 5, 1993, reflected that Paul Shrader unit #271 at 2:41 P.M. checked Larry Ceaser, radio log reflected #271 Sharder was in the South East Part of West Memphis, Larry Ceaser stated he remembed the white police checking him last month & they checked him in front of the police substation in the Project. Larry Ceasers denies every being at Bojangles on MO Street. [signed] Michael W. Allen

06/28/93 Michael Scott 301 S. 20th B/M was talked to by Sgt. Mike Allen. Michael Scott had on his arm a permanent cast on his right arm & a cast on his left arm. Hasn't had a temporary brace blue in color with velcro white stripes. Has had cast on right arm plaster white prior to May 5th 1993 & received injury to left arm May 16th 1993. (Police report on File) Denies being at Bojangles ever. (Manager of Bojangles stated the Black Male was somewhat mentally ill & that brace was not plaster but Blue Material type with White Velcro stripes.) As of 6/28/93 the black male described at Bojangle's hadn't been identified. [signed] Mike Allen

Marty King testified that he had never been approached by the police again regarding this incident. The blood samples taken by the police were declared lost.

Was Mr. Bojangles involved in the murders of the children? Perhaps the most interesting facts about him were that even though he was bleeding and disoriented, he did not seek assistance. He did not come forward later to explain his actions, in spite of his notoriety. It appears as though he was avoiding authorities, perhaps his injuries were related to criminal activity, and perhaps he had an active warrant for his arrest.

It is rightly pointed out that Mr. Bojangles could not have likely have been a sole perpetrator or could have walked all the way bleeding and disoriented from the Blue Beacon area without leaving more of a trail of blood. This consideration has the Blue Beacon woods as the site of the murders. Perhaps the murders took place in a location nearer to the Bojangles restaurant. Perhaps Mr. Bojangles had a falling out and fight with the other perpetrators. Or, quite possibly, this event had nothing to do with the murders. All of these remain as speculation, as the mystery of Mr. Bojangles has never been solved.

The Tattooed Man

Perhaps as unsettling as the Bojangles incident is the account of a mysterious hitchhiker sometimes called "the tattooed man." Ken Govar was travelling east on I-40 when he picked up a hitchhiker on the road about 20 miles outside of Little Rock. The man told Govar that he was heading to Knoxville, Tennessee. He was described as intense, and angry. But what was most unnerving to Govar, was a large tattoo of a devil on the passenger's forearm. When they arrived in West Memphis at 3:30 pm, the hitchhiker insisted on being left there, even though Govar told him that he would be able to take him further along the way to Knoxville. He asked to be let out at a convenience store on the south side of the interstate. From the description given by Govar, this store would either have been directly next to the Blue Beacon or further down next to 18th Street. Both locations would put him within walking distance to The Robin Hood Hills area. Ken Govar gave an interview to the Little Rock Police and they made a sketch of the individual and the tattoo.

". . . on the forearm of his left arm, he had
a 6" to 8" tattoo of a devil sitting on its
haunches with three claws up on his hands
and the face, looked like kinda dinosaur
sitting there on his haunches, with the three
claws up like this but he had the face of a
traditional devil, like you would draw a
devil with a pointed chin and you know the
horns and everything. . . . It was horrible."

The hitchhiker's description given to police by Govar:

26 to 28 years old

5'8 to 5'10

"On the thin side of thin"

Reddish blonde hair, bushy eyebrows and sideburns

Stubbly red beard

Freckles

Bone tattoo in blood red background on right forearm.

Devil tattoo on left forearm

Worked trimming trees

The police made a file with the sketches and the notes from Govar. He said that he was never contacted again by the West Memphis police.

In the door to door interviews, one woman described someone with a devil tattoo. She talked about the Wren twins, who at age 19 already had served jail time and had a prison break to their names. "The Wren boys have dropped out of sight last couple of days! A boy & girl have been in the neighborhood for the Wren boy's. This boy has a tattoo on his left forearm of a devil with a hood on! With scratches on chest! Jeff." (The exclamation marks were in the original police notes.) She went on to describe Jeff as a white male, 5'9, 180, 18 years of age with a yellow Monte Carlo.

The police interviewed a Jeff Looney, who in some ways fit this description. He knew the Wrens, having dated one of their sisters. His father owned a "butterscotch" colored Fifth Avenue, a car that is large and boxy just like a

Monte Carlo. He was on the thin side of thin, 5'11 and 140. He had a job trimming bushes. He had a number of tattoos and his arms were photographed. However, none of the tattoos looked like a devil.

The sketch made by Govar looks like the suspect, William Welch. According to his intake form, Welch did have a Grim Reaper tattoo on his left arm and a rose and heart on his right. He was 5'10 and 160, but he could be better described as muscular rather than thin. His hair was sandy blonde.

But could either of these have been the tattooed man? The only link in the West Memphis police files was Govar's sketch, and it found its way into the jacket of another mysterious individual. On May the 6th, someone had taken a cab from Memphis to Centerville, Tennessee, 168 miles. At first, he asked to go to a hotel near the airport and then asked to be driven to Nashville. He got out of the cab in Centerville, Tennessee when the driver was refueling.

Tracy Laxton was brought in to the police because he had frightened several local teenagers (including Jessie Misskelley). Based on the fact that Tracy Laxton admitted to hitching rides and returning to town recently and the fact that he had red hair was 5'7 and 140 pounds he was included in the line-up, although his heavy facial hair probably excluded him. Govar said that none of the men matched the person who he remembered and that the tattoo was definitely a devil, and not a grim reaper.

When John Mark Byers arrived home at 11:00 p.m., he called the Sheriff to request a search and rescue team. He said, *"Look, I've had one police officer out here helping me look for these boys. Now, I called once and*

ya'll told me what to do, and I did that. Now I'm calling now, and I want to know why the search and rescue squad won't come out here and help me look for my boy." He was then told to call Denver Reed, the leader of the Crittenden County team the following morning.

John and Ryan left the house again and drove to the Blue Beacon Truck Wash. Here he told the people inside that he was looking for his son Chris and two other boys. He then drove around the back. For some time, Byers and Ryan shouted for the boys and honked their horn. Still unable to find the boys, they drove back home.

The Blue Beacon Truck Wash

They were met there by Melissa, Terry Hobbs, Steven Branch's grandfather, and Diana Moore. After a short discussion, the group decided to make another attempt to search for the boys in the woods.

CHAPTER TWO
MAY 6TH 1993
MURDER IN ROBIN
HOOD HILLS

WARNING
This chapter contains graphic photos
of the crime scene and the victims.

At 1:30 a.m., May 6th, Sergeant Ball of the West Memphis Police Department (WMPD), drove to the Byers's home to inform John and Melissa that a search for the boys was being conducted in the area. After he left at about 2:00 a.m., Tony Hudson, a friend of Byers, came to the house. Byers and Hudson left soon after to search the Mid-Continent building which was currently vacant and being rebuilt after having been blown over in a recent storm. They thought that the boys may have been hiding there. When John and Tony arrived, they saw a black van nearby. It was locked and they assumed that it belonged to one of the workers at the site. They continued their search for about an hour before they returned home with the intention of resuming their search as soon as it was daylight.

The next morning John Byers called Denver Reed and arranged to meet him at 8:00 a.m. The search resumed in the Robin Hood Hills area, with Terry Hobbs, Diana Moore, Byers and a number of others. After John met with Reed, another search was conducted until 1:45 p.m. when Sergeant Mike Allen found the first body of the missing boys. The exact circumstances behind the discovery of the children are a bit vague. The initial police statements referred to Officer Mike Allen finding a floating tennis shoe in the ditch in the Blue Beacon Woods. Because of the snafu that no detectives were notified until early morning on May 6th, detectives were trudging through the crime scene they did not yet know was a crime scene; until Detective Mike Allen saw the unmistakable yellow Cub Scout hat and a child's sneaker floating in the stream.

Later this was amended to say that it was a juvenile probation officer that found the floating shoe. On scene at the time of the discovery of the children were: Steve Jones, probation officer; Mike Allen, detective West Memphis Police; Diane Hester, West Memphis Police; George Phillips, West Memphis Police; and, Billy Sanders, West Memphis Police.

While Mike Allen attempted to retrieve the items by leaning over the creek with his hands on a tree on the opposite side, he lost his footing on the muddy bank and slid into the murky aquatic coffin of the missing boys.

Allen's foot slid underneath the first victim, and caused the naked, hog-tied and badly bruised body of Michael Moore to float to the surface at approximately 1 PM.

Although the unsigned police report doesn't state the exact location of the discovery, it implies that the body was found submerged in a creek about 60 yards south of Interstate 55. An hour later, the body was removed from the creek by police officers.

Shortly after the first victim's body was removed, the second body was found by Detective Bryn Ridge, then the third another five feet away. Chris Byers and Steve Branch were found face down and fully submerged and were located by the apparent purposeful placement of sticks jammed into the mud. The sticks had items of the boys clothing wrapped around the bottom ends.

Byers and Branch were also found totally naked, hog-tied and badly beaten; Stevie sustained significant gouging wounds to the left of his face and Chris was emasculated.

Despite the fact that the coroner was two hours away, all three victims were removed from the ditch and placed on the banks. They were all covered by black plastic while the WMPD continued to collect evidence from the scene. County workers were enlisted to pump out the stream.

Twenty minutes after the third body was located, the WMPD contacted Crittenden County Coroner, Ken Hale. The police informed him that the bodies were found in the woods behind the Blue Beacon Truck

Wash. By 4:00 p.m., Hale had pronounced all three of the boys dead.

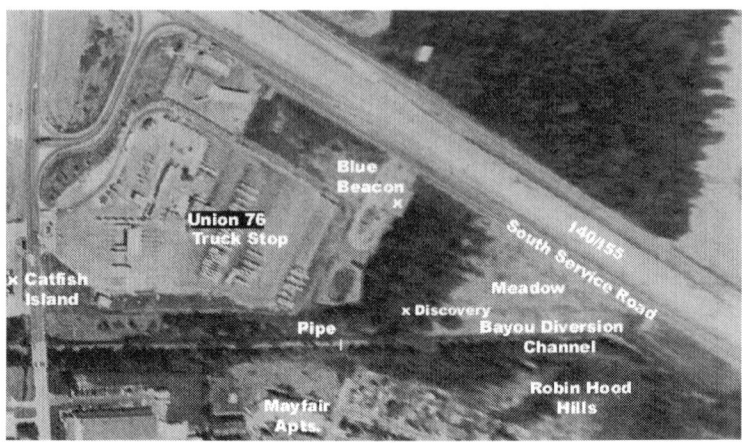

This was from a police photo. The entrance to Robin Hood Hills is where the victims were last seen. Catfish Island is the workplace of Pamela Hobbs and where she was when she was notified the children were missing. The discovery site was separated from the Robin Hood Hills by the Bayou Diversion Channel.

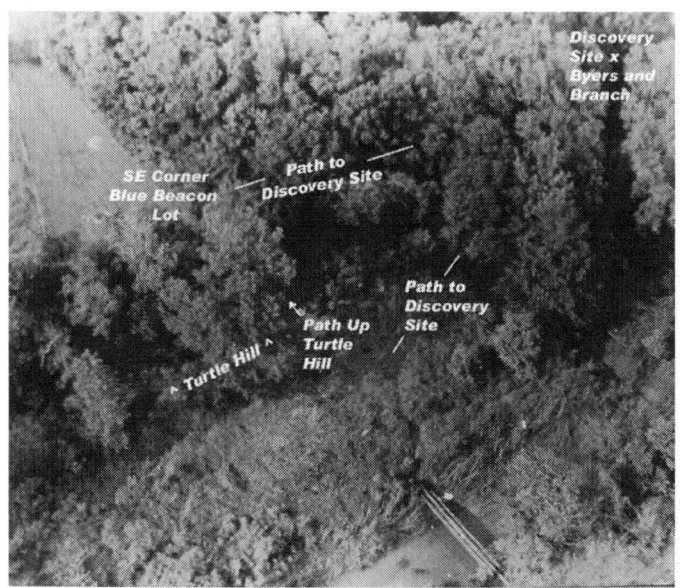

A closer view of the discovery site

Crittenden County juvenile probation officer Steve Jones suggested detectives speak to a local teen that just might know something about these crimes. His name was Damien Echols. The next day Lt James Sudbury and Steve Jones paid Echols a visit.

By the morning of May 7th, the small town of West Memphis was rocked by the news of the discovery of the mutilated bodies of three eight-year-old boys. Rumors spread like wildfire regarding the nature of the murders through the small tight knit town. It was soon well known that the boys had been cut with a knife, raped and at least one of the boy's genitals had been cut. Many of these rumors were based on inaccurate police assumptions and media hype.

Unfortunately, the misinformation about the facts of this case would sway the community into believing that these were satanic cult killings. And it did not take long for this small community to start a good old Salem style witch hunt.

By noon, police were questioning their first suspect, Damien Echols. Some believed that he was a suspect based only on the fact that he "looked" like someone who could commit a crime like this. He had black hair, wore black clothing and listened to heavy metal music. In the small town of West Memphis, this was enough to take all the focus off of the rest of the community and only focus on Damien Echols.

Sudbury and Jones arrived at 2706 South Grove in Broadway Trailer Park in West Memphis, Arkansas, where Echols lived. They talked briefly with Damien's mother, Pamela Hutcheson, and father, Eddie Hutcheson and gained their permission to interview Damien. They conducted this initial interview in Damien's bedroom. At that time, Lieutenant Sudbury took a Polaroid photograph of Damien Echols and noted that he had a tattoo on his chest of a five-pointed star or pentagram and another unidentified tattoo on his shoulder or arm. When the interview was completed no charges were filed but Damien Echols was still a suspect.

Here is transcript of the police Lt. James Sudbury's report on that first meeting with Damien.

On the day after the bodies of the three boys were found I had a conversation with Steve Jones, a Juvenile Officer for Crittenden County, Arkansas. In our conversation I found that Steve and I shared the same opinion that the murders appeared to have overtones of a cult sacrifice.

During our conversation Steve mentioned that of all the people known by him to be involved in cult type activities one person stood out in his mind that in his opinion was capable of being involved in this type of crime. That person was Damien Echols. Steve stated that Damien lived at 2706 South Grove in Broadway Trailer park in West Memphis, Arkansas. On this day, the day after the bodies were found, I asked Steve if he would meet me at Damien's residence in order to interview Damien.

In fact the day after the bodies were discovered I went to 2706 South Grove and meet with Steve Jones whereas we talked to Pamela and Eddie Hutcheson the mother and step-father of Damien. Neither Pamela or Eddie objected to our talking to Damien. On this day, with Pamela and Eddie's permission, we talked to Damien in his bed room and on this day I took a Polaroid of Damien Echols. At this time I observed Damien to have a tattoo on his chest of a five pointed star or pentagram and as best I remember one other tattoo on his shoulder or arm. I am unsure of the nature of this tattoo.

[signed] Lt. James Sudbury.

The official autopsy reports submitted by Dr. Frank J Peretti, of the Arkansas State Crime Laboratory, and Kent Hale described the condition of the boys as they were found on the afternoon of May 6th 1993. The initial conclusion, drawn by police at the scene, was that the boys had been raped but this was not verified by the autopsy. The dilation of the anus was wrongly believed to have been evidence of anal rape, but it is, in fact, a natural occurrence at death. Although there was no evidence to suggest that all three of the boys had been sexually assaulted, Hale stated in his report that this may have been a possibility.

NOTE each child's autopsy report is 8-9 pages long. We omitted the entire report and just added the Medical Examiner's final overview of the autopsy. (Also known as the OPINION)

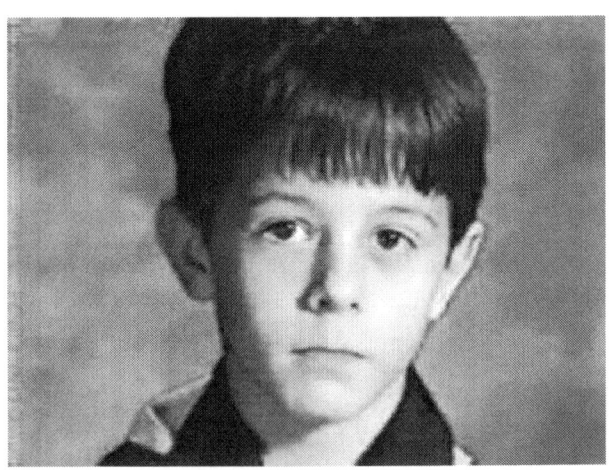

Michael Moore

James M. Moore had died of multiple traumatic injuries to the head, torso, and extremities with drowning. He had been found in a drainage ditch and had drowned in two feet of water. He had been found completely nude, with his wrists bound to his ankles by shoelaces. There was little evidence that showed that he had defended himself against his attacker(s) and the lack of injuries caused by the ligatures suggests that he had not struggled after he was tied up. This would suggest that he was unconscious at an early stage in the attack. There was no evidence of sexual assault.

ARKANSAS STATE CRIME LABORATORY MEDICAL EXAMINER DIVISION

Case No.: ME-329-93 Date of Examination: May 7, 1993
Name: MOORE, James Michael
Age: 8 years Race: White Sex: Male
Place of Death: West Memphis, Arkansas
County: Crittenden
CONCLUSIONS
CAUSE OF DEATH: Multiple Injuries with

Drowning.

MANNER OF DEATH: Homicide.

LABORATORY RESULTS

TOXICOLOGY:

Ethyl Alcohol: Blood -- <0.01g%

Drug Screen: Blood-- No drugs detected.

SEROLOGY:

Blood Type: A+

Frank J. Peretti, M.D. * William Q. Sturner, M.D.

Assoc. Medical Examiner Chief Medical Examiner

*Pathologist of Record

05-25-93/tjg

OPINION:

This 8 year old white male, James Michael Moore, died of multiple injuries with drowning.

Investigation of the circumstances of death revealed that the decedent was one of three children (see related cases MEA-330-93 and

MEA-331-93) that were found in a ditch which contained approximately 2 to 2 _ feet of water, approximately 150 yards southwest of Blue Beacon Truck Wash on the south service of road at Interstate 40 and 55, West Memphis, Arkansas. The decadent was reported missing at approximately 6:00 PM on May 5, 1993 and his nude body was found the afternoon of May 6, 1993. When found the body was nude and the wrists were bound to the ankles bilaterally.

Autopsy showed that the decadent's hands were bound to his feet in a "hog-tied" fashion. There were multiple traumatic injuries consisting of contusions, abrasions, and lacerations involving the head, torso, and extremities. The skull showed multiple fractures with associated brain injury. Defense type injuries consisting of cuts were present on the hands. The anus was dilated and contained mud. Spermatozoa were not detected in the oral and anal smears. In addition, there was evidence of drowning, which included "washerwoman" wrinkling of the hands, pulmonary edema and congestion, aspiration of water into the sphenoid sinus and petechial hemorrhages involving the heart, lung and thymus. The alcohol detected is probably the result of decomposition. No drugs were identified in the body fluids.

MANNER OF DEATH: Homicide.

Frank J. Peretti, M.D. William Q. Sturner, M.D.
Assoc. Medical Examiner Chief Medical Examiner
*Pathologist of Record

Steven Branch

Steven Branch died of multiple traumatic injuries to the head, torso, and extremities with drowning. He had been found in the drainage ditch near the bodies of James Moore and Christopher Byers, in two feet of water. As with the other two victims, he was found naked, with his wrists bound to his ankles by shoelaces. There were many violent, traumatic injuries to Steven's face and head, along with a number of superficial scratches, abrasions, and contusions over the rest of his body. While the wounds were similar to those found on James, they were much more intense. There was also a three-inch fracture at the base of the skull. Peretti did not note the presence of extensive defensive wounds. Although there was no evidence to support this, Hale, in his report, stated that Steven may have been sexually assaulted.

ARKANSAS STATE CRIME LABORATORY MEDICAL EXAMINER DIVISION

Case No.: ME-330-93 Date of Examination: May 7, 1993
Name: BRANCH, Steve Edward
Age: 8 years Race: White Sex: Male
Place of Death: West Memphis, Arkansas
County: Crittenden
CONCLUSIONS
CAUSE OF DEATH: Multiple Injuries with Drowning.
MANNER OF DEATH: Homicide.
LABORATORY RESULTS
TOXICOLOGY:
Ethyl Alcohol: None detected in Blood.

Acid and Neutral Drugs: None detected in Blood.
Basic Drugs: None detected in Blood.
SEROLOGY:
Blood Type: A+

Frank J. Peretti, M.D.* William Q. Sturner
Assoc. Medical Examiner Chief Medical
Examiner
*Pathologist of Record
05-24-93/tjg

OPINION:
This 8 year old, white male, Steve Branch, died of multiple injuries with drowning. Investigation of the circumstances of death revealed that the decedent was one of three children (see related cases MEA-329-93 and MEA-331-93) that were found in a ditch which contained approximately 2 to 2 _ feet of water, approximately 150 yards southwest of Blue Beacon Truck Wash on the south service road at Interstate 40 and 55, West Memphis, Arkansas. The decadent was

reported missing at approximately 6:00 PM on May 5, 1993, and his body was found the afternoon of May 6, 1993. When found the body was nude and the wrists were bound the ankles bilaterally.

Autopsy demonstrated multiple cutting and gouging wounds and abrasions involving the facies. There were fractures of the base of the skull and hemorrhage involving the brain. There were multiple contusions, abrasions, and lacerations involving the torso and extremities. The penis showed injuries consisting of segmental intense hyperemia involving the mid shaft, glans and head of the penis with overlying very fine scratches. There was evidence also of terminal submersion consistent with "washerwoman" wrinkling of the hands and feet. There was pulmonary edema and congestion, along with the bloody, frothy fluid, in the air passages and water in the sphenoid sinus. Petechial hemorrhages were present on the epicardium and pleura. The anus was dilated, with no external evidence of injury. The anal and rectal mucosae were slightly hyperemic and showed no injuries. Spermatoza were not identified on the oral and anal smears. No drugs or alcohol were detected in the body fluids.

MANNER OF DEATH: Homicide.

Frank J. Peretti, M.D.* William Q. Sturner Assoc. Medical Examiner Chief Medical Examiner
*Pathologist of Record

Christopher Byers

Christopher Byers received the most extensive, violent and most overtly sexual injuries of the three victims. He died of multiple traumatic injuries to the head, as well as the violent removal of his penis, the scrotal sac, and the testes, along with associated cuts and stab wounds to the genital area. He was found in the same drainage ditch as James and Steven. He was completely naked, with his wrists bound to his ankles by shoelaces. The toxicology report also revealed non-therapeutic levels of the drug Carbamazepine in the blood. There were also a variety of healed injuries. Peretti noted that there were defensive wounds. There were also three sets of wounds on the buttocks. While this attack was sexual in nature, there is no evidence of rape, although, Hale did state that this was a possibility. Christopher Byers did not drown as he was already dead before being placed in the water.

ARKANSAS STATE CRIME LABORATORY MEDICAL EXAMINER DIVISION

Case No.: ME-331-93 Date of Examination: May 7, 1993
Name: BYERS, Christopher Mark
Age: 8 years Race: White Sex: Male
Place of Death: West Memphis, Arkansas
County: Crittenden
CONCLUSIONS
CAUSE OF DEATH: Multiple Injuries.
MANNER OF DEATH: Homicide.
LABORATORY RESULTS
TOXICOLOGY:
Ethyl Alcohol: Blood—Negative
Drug Screens: Blood—Acid & Neutral
Drugs—5.737 ug/ml Carbamazepine

Basic Drugs—None Detected
SEROLOGY:
Blood Type: O+
Oral smear/swabs: No semen found
Rectal smears/swabs: No semen or blood found.

Frank J. Peretti, M.D. * William Q. Sturner Assoc. Medical Examiner Chief Medical Examiner
*Pathologist of Record
05-28-93/tjg

OPINION:
This 8 year old, white male, Christopher Byers, dies of multiple injuries.
Investigation of the three circumstances of death revealed that the decadent was one of three children (see related cases MEA-329-93 and MEA-330-93) that were found in a ditch which contained approximately 2 to 2 1/2 feet of water, approximately 150 yards

southwest of Blue Beacon Truck Wash on the south service road at Interstate 40 and 55, West Memphis, Arkansas. The decadent was reported missing at approximately 6:00 PM on May 5, 1993 and his nude body was found the afternoon of May 6, 1993. When found the body was nude and the wrists were bound to the ankles bilaterally.

Autopsy demonstrated bindings of the hands and feet behind the back in a "hog-tied" fashion with shoe laces. There were multiple abrasions, contusions and lacerations of the facies which resulted in hemorrhage and fracturing of the skull. The skin of the penis, scrotal sac and testes, were missing. Surrounding the perineum were multiple cutting wounds. The anus was dilated with a hyperemic mucosa. There were no injuries present. Spermatoza were not detected in the oral and anal smears. In addition, there were multiple and extensive contusions, abrasions, and lacerations involving the torso and extremities. No alcohol was detected. Carbamazepine was detected in sub-therapeutic levels.

MANNER OF DEATH: Homicide

Frank J. Peretti, M.D.* William Q. Sturner Assoc. Medical Examiner Chief Medical Examiner
*Pathologist of Record

Hale's report stated that lividity (the red discoloration in the skin caused by the pooling and settling of blood within the blood vessels after death) was present in all three victims and blanched with pressure. Lividity begins about 30 minutes after death and then fixes, after four or five hours blanching no longer occurs, depending on environmental conditions. According to this, the time of death could be placed at some time after daybreak on 6 May 1993, although this is difficult to ascertain as the victim's body temperatures were not taken.

It was found that rigor mortis, the stiffening of the muscle tissue, which begins after death, was present in all three victims. Rigor mortis begins about two to four hours after death, and full rigor mortis is complete eight to 12 hours after death, depending on environmental conditions. According to Hale, it was difficult to determine whether rigor mortis was complete due to the manner in which the boys were tied, but Peretti stated in his report that rigor was evenly present throughout the extremities.

Arial view of site where bodies were
found
A. Truck stop car park
B. Truck wash
C. Trail
D. Pipe where bikes were found
E. Site where boys' bodies were found

After a thorough search of the area there was no murder weapon found at the scene with the bodies. The boy's bicycles and clothing were dumped in the drainage ditch with the bodies, effectively removing any trace evidence which may have been present. The clothing had been held down with sticks but these were not collected by police at the time. Six months later they would find two sticks in the woods, and claim that they were the sticks found at the scene. It was also determined that two pairs of the boys' underwear were missing. The only signs of blood at the crime scene were where the bodies had rested on the bank after their removal from the water, and some blood in the water. Because of this there was no blood evidence collected. Luminol testing was done on May 12th. At the time Luminol testing was not admissible in court. An area on the bank had been deliberately cleared and two imprints of a tennis shoe were found.

Tennis shoe imprint found at the scene

Second tennis shoe imprint found

CHAPTER THREE
ALIBIS AND
FAIRYTALES

Damien Echols

The first person that the authorities focused their attention on was Damien Echols. Some feel that the only reason that the police focused on Damien was the fact that he "looked" like the type of person that would commit a crime like this. And this was widely portrayed by the local media and

John Mark Byers, the father of Christopher Byers.

In 2014, a retired NYPD homicide detective went to West Memphis and looked into the facts surrounding the case and talked to people close to the investigation in 1993. Three former WMPD officers where asked if their investigation and arrest of Damien was based solely on the idea that Damien was a worshiper of Satan. All three agreed that the Satan worshiping concept was mainly a ploy used by the media to keep the attention on the case and to sell papers. At no time was the investigation hanging its entire case on the "satanic worship" concept.

One retired officer commented, *"It was the statements that Damien told us that we were able to prove during our investigation to be lies that kept our focus on him. He had no alibi what so ever for the night the boys came up missing. He lied about the phone call with Holly George, a credible eye witness placed Damien in the neighborhood on the afternoon of the killings and on top of all of that he failed the lie detector test. But the media did not want to report any of this information because it would turn the case into a legitimate murder case and that does not sell papers."*

It was true, evidence and statements that pointed to the possibility of Damien, Jason and Jessie being guilty was kept out of the public's eye. In most investigations some of the information is withheld by the police and the State attorney's office for the reason of building their case for trial. But in this case, the media totally ignored the evidence or statements that pointed at the guilt of these three men.

Before we look at the statements and evidence let's look at who Damien Echols really is.

Damien is the son of Pam and Eddie Hutchison. He was named Michael Wayne Hutchison at birth. Damien's father left the family after he got his first and only moderate paying job. Jack Echols, Pam's second husband, adopted Damien and his sister Constance Michelle.

At the time of the adoption, Damien was very involved in the Catholic Church, and was going over different names of the saints. St. Michael's was where he went to church. He heard about this man from the Hawaiian Islands, Father Damien, that took care of lepers until he finally caught the disease himself and died. Damien said that he changed his name to "Damien" after this beloved priest.

According to medical and social records, Jack Echols sexually abused Michelle and was verbally and physically abusive to the entire family. Pam eventually left Jack and resumed her relationship with Damien's biological father Eddie Hutchison in the months before the murders. Their rented trailer had one working door and no bedroom for Damien.

The home of Damien Echols in May 1993

There are no elementary school records for Damien, and by both parents accounts, he lived his early childhood in a shack in the middle of a field with no water or electricity.

In the 18 months prior to the murders, Damien was arrested for trespassing, sexual misconduct and committed to a psychiatric hospital.

He was suspended from school seven times the year before, once for lighting a fire in the back of class, the last time because he clawed the face of Shane Divilbiss, a romantic rival for the affections of Deanna

Holcomb, who was arrested with Damien a few months later.

Damien's last commitment, while living with the recently relocated family in Aloha Oregon, was caused by Echols threatening to slit his mother's throat and drink her blood, and subsequently eat his father.

Pam and Eddie Hutchison were so concerned about Damien's behavior and his threats to them that they refused to allow him back into the home and sent him on a bus back to Arkansas to live with his adoptive father, Jack Echols.

About seven months prior to the murders Damien reportedly killed a Great Dane that was sick. A witness to the killing stated that Damien hit the dog in the back of the head and after the dog was dead he pulled the dog's intestines out and stomped on the dog until blood came out of its mouth. It was also reported that Damien also planned on saving the skull of the dead dog.

Here is the eyewitness report of Joe Houston who was present on the day that the dog was killed.

Statement of: Joe Houston Bartoush, Jr.
Route 2 Box 767 Lakeshore

DOB **-**-80 ***-****

On 10-27-92 I was at Lakeshore Trailer Park with Damien Echols when he killed a Black Great Dane. The dog was already sick and he hit the dog in the back of the head. He pulled the intestines out of the dog and started stomping the dog until blood came out of his mouth. He was going to come back later with battery acid so that he could burn the hair and skin off of the dog's head. He had two cat skulls, a dog skull and a rat skull that I already knew about. He kept these skulls in his bedroom at Jack Echols house in Lakeshore. He was trying to make the eyeballs of the dog he killed pop out when he was stomping. Damien had a camouflage survival knife to cut the guts out of the dog with. This statement was written by Det. Ridge at my request.

This statement was completed at 2:07 PM on the 14 day of June 1993.

Witness: Det. B. Ridge
X Joe Bartoush(Signature of person giving voluntary statement)

Witness: Hubert B. Bartoush

The Hutchison's moved back to West Memphis six weeks before the murders and Damien moved back in with them. Damien is suspected to have burned down his adoptive father Jack Echols' garage and part of his trailer according to his friend Chris Littrell.

According to Damien's OWN application for Social Security disability benefits, he was suffering from homicidal, sociopathic and suicidal ideations, manic depression and schizophrenia:

The exhibit known as the "500", as in 500 pages of medical records tells the story the prosecution could not, due to the exclusion of "prior bad acts". There was great concern about Damien's escalating propensity for violence, so much so his probation officer removed the dog and cat skulls from his bedroom and expressed and great concern for acts against others. Eighteen months prior to the murders he felt the natural evolution of his violence was going to be against humans.

Damien was told at the hospital that he could be the next Ted Bundy. He replied, "I always knew".

In her first police interview, Damien's mother, Pam tells WMPD that her husband had packed up and left her the night before the three young boys went missing, and took everything to his mother's by 9:00 PM.

Pam described Damien as upset and crying over the incident.

In her subsequent deposition in September 1993, she recants this happened on this evening. Pam told detectives that Damien was normal, and that he had no problems. It was not until detectives prompted her that they knew of his hospitalizations through his probation officer that she even admitted he was on medication.

HUTCHISON: I THINK HE'S A PRETTY DECENT YOUNG MAN, I'VE NEVER HAD ANY PROBLEMS WITH HIM.

HUTCHISON: NO, HE WASN'T FAIRLY NORMAL, HE WAS, HE WAS MUCH BETTER THAN NORMAL.

SUDBURY: SO AS FOR AS DISCIPLINED?

HUTCHISON: *HE WAS NEVER DISCIPLINED PROBLEM, NO*

May 9th & 10th Interviews

On May 9th Detective Bill Durham and Shane Griffin spoke to Damien, Domini and Jason in Jason's front yard. The interview was cut short when Jason's mother arrived home.

NOTES ON INTERVIEWS WITH ECHOLS, TEER, AND BALDWIN (DETECTIVE BILL DURHAM, MAY 9, 1993)

On May 9, 1993, Shane Griffin and I talked with Damien Echols, Domini Teer and Jason Baldwin at 5:00PM, in the front yard at Jason Baldwin's house at 245 W. Lake Dr. S., Lake Shore.

They said that on Wednesday, 5-5-93 that they had gone to Jason's uncle's house and Jason had cut the lawn. Unsure of time they went or address. It is somewhere off Dover behind Blockbuster Video. Damien phoned his father to pick them up at the Laundromat at Missouri and N. Worthington. They said they were picked up at 6:00PM and Damien's father took Jason and Domini home and Damien went home.

Shane Griffin, at this time started asking the questions on the sheet (questionnaire) and did complete the sheet on Damien. He was asking Jason the questions when Jason Baldwin's mother arrived. We were standing in the front yard at Jason Baldwin's house trailer. Mrs. Baldwin was very upset and accused us of picking on her son and said she did not want us talking to him. I attempted to reason with her but to no avail. We then left.

Later an official interview with Damien was conducted. During this interview Damien was asked whether one of the boys was more savagely attacked than the other two, to which Damien told them that he believed one of the boys had been mutilated more than the others and had his genitals cut. Police considered that this was information that would only have been known by the killer(s). The prosecution later used this statement to support their case that Damien had prior knowledge of the crimes that was not generally available.

The following report is from the records of the West Memphis Police Department. No changes have been made to the report and any typos are part of the original report. Any notes from the authors are notated with the heading ***NOTES*** and are put in to the report with *italics* to separate the information from the original report.

INVESTIGATIVE REPORT (May 10, 1993)

TRIPLE HOMICIDE

BYERS/MOORE/BRANCH

CASE FILE NUMBER 93050666

DATE OF REPORT: 05-10-93

Polygraph Test and Report

ON 05-10-93, DAMIEN WAYNE ECHOLS WHO IS ALSO KNOWN AS MICHAEL WAYNE HUTCHISON CAME TO THE WEST MEMPHIS POLICE DEPARTMENT FOR AN INTERVIEW CONCERNING ANY INFORMATION THAT HE MAY HAVE CONCERNING THE ABOVE NOTED HOMICIDE. PRESENT DURING THE INTERVIEW WERE LT. JAMES SUDBURY OF THE CRITTENDEN COUNTY DRUG TASK FORCE, MYSELF DETECTIVE B. RIDGE, AND DAMIEN. A SUBJECT DESCRIPTION WAS FILLED OUT THAT CONTAINED INFORMATION ABOUT DAMIEN'S RESIDENCE, HIS VITAL STATISTICS, AND HIS FAMILY. AT THIS POINT DAMIEN WAS NOT CONSIDERED TO BE A SUSPECT AND ONLY GENERAL KNOWLEDGE QUESTIONS WERE BEING ASKED. DAMIEN WAS VERY CALM AND EVEN COLD AS HE ANSWERED THE QUESTIONS CONCERNING HIS BACKGROUND AND ANY KNOWLEDGE HE MAY HAVE HAD CONCERNING THE HOMICIDE.

DAMIEN STATED THAT HE WAS A
MEMBER OF A WHITE WITCH GROUP
THAT HE REFERRED TO AS WICCA.
HE STATED THAT HIS BELIEF WAS
THERE WAS A GODDESS AND NOT A
GOD. HE STATED THAT EVERYONE IN
THE GROUP WORKS TOWARD A
DIVINE LIGHT UPON REACHING THAT
STATE THEY BECOME LIKE GODS
THEMSELVES. HE HAS BEEN A
MEMBER OF THIS GROUP FOR ABOUT
5 YEARS HE STATED.

DAMIEN STATED THAT HE HAD MET
ONE PERSON THAT HE CONSIDERED
TO BE A PRIESTESS. HE STATED THAT
THE PERSON HE MET WAS DEANNA
HOLCOME WHO HE STATED LIVED IN
THE HARBOR YARD, HARDIN
VILLAGE AREA OF MARION ON
CABRALE COVE. HE STATED THAT
SHE WORSHIPPED CATS IN WHAT
SHE DID WITH HER FORM OF
WITCHCRAFT.

DAMIEN STATED THAT ON TUESDAY
050493 HE WAS AT HOME FROM

WHEN HE GOT OUT OF BED AT
ABOUT 10:30 TO 11:00 A.M UNTIL HE
GOT UP AT ABOUT 12:00 NOON WHEN
HE LEFT AND WENT TO LAKESHORE.
HE STATED THAT HE HAS A LOT OF
FRIENDS AT LAKESHORE SINCE HE
USED TO LIVE THERE WITH HIS
STEPFATHER JACK ECHOLS.

DAMIEN WAS WEARING A NECKLACE
THAT HE CLAIMED THAT HE HAD
JUST BOUGHT AT THE MALL OF
MEMPHIS ON THE SATURDAY
BEFORE THIS INTERVIEW. THE
NECKLACE HAD A PENTAGRAM AS A
PENDANT THAT DAMIEN EXPLAINED
MEANT SOME TYPE OF GOOD
SYMBOL FOR THE WICCA MAGIC
THAT HE WAS IN.

DAMIEN STATED THAT ON
WEDNESDAY HE WAS WITH JASON
BALDWIN AND DOMINI TEER AND
THAT THEY HAD GONE TO JASON'S
UNCLE'S HOUSE ON CENTER STREET
IN WEST MEMPHIS. HE COULDN'T
GIVE A SPECIFIC ADDRESS BUT SAID

THAT IT WAS NEAR ALEXANDER'S LAUNDRY MAT WHERE HE STATED THAT HE CALLED HIS MOTHER TO PICK HIM UP.

NOTE

Jason's uncle Hubert Bartoush said in a statement that Jason was at his home alone on the May 5th. And the time frame that Jason was at his uncle's house does not tie into the time frame that Damien stated. Jason was at the home of Hubert Bartoush from about 4:30 PM to about 6:30 PM. Damien later states that he was at the home of Susan Sanders from about 3:00 to 5:00 PM. He also stated that after leaving the home of Susan Sanders he went home.

STATEMENT OF: Hubert B. Bartoush
DATE: PAGE:
1037 Park W. Mphs.
DOB: 10-3-29 S/R [omitted]

On 5-5-93 Jason Baldwin, my Grand Nephew, came to my house at about 4:30 PM and mowed my yard. He was alone when he was at my house. He left my house at about 6:30 PM and said he was going to Walmart to play video games. I remember the times because Jeopardy was coming on when he got here and Wheel of Fortune was coming on when he left.

I have written this statement consisting of 1 page[s], and I affirm to the truth and accuracy of the facts contained therein.

This statement was completed at 1:56 PM., on the 14 day of June 1993.

WITNESS: Det. B. Ridge
Hubert B. Bartoush
WITNESS: Signature of person giving voluntary statement

HE STATED THAT HIS MOTHER PICKED HIM UP ALONG WITH DOMINI TEER AND TOOK DOMINI HOME. DOMINI IS DAMIEN'S GIRLFRIEND WHO IS PREGNANT WITH DAMIEN'S BABY. DOMINI LIVES IN LAKESHORE TRAILER PARK WITH HER MOTHER.

DAMIEN STATED THAT AFTER HE AND HIS MOTHER DROPPED DOMINI OFF THAT HE ALONG WITH HIS MOTHER, SISTER (MICHELLE), AND FATHER (JOE HUTCHISON) HAD GONE TO THE RESIDENCE OF SUSAN SANDERS AND VISITED FOR A WHILE. HE STATED THAT HE WAS AT THEIR RESIDENCE AT ABOUT 3:00 TO 5:00 PM ON THAT DATE AND AFTER LEAVING THE RESIDENCE HE WENT HOME WHERE HE STATED THAT HE GOT ON THE PHONE WITH A HOLLY GEORGE WHO HE STATES LIVES IN BARTLETT, TENNESSEE. HE STATED THAT HE GOT OFF OF THE TELEPHONE WITH HOLLY AFTER TALKING FOR A LONG TIME AT ABOUT 11:30 PM THAT NIGHT.

*** *NOTE* ***

Holly George was interviewed on September 10th and Damien's statement conflicted with the statement that Holly had made regarding the time and length of the phone call. Damien stated that he called

Holly after he got home (after 5 PM) and that he was on the phone with her for a long time and got off the phone about 11:30 PM.

Here is the partial transcript from the interview with Holly George.

RIDGE: OKAY, SO YOU TRIED TO CALL JASON THAT DAY AND YOU COULDN'T ANSWER AND THAT WAS SHORTLY AFTER YOU HAD TALKED TO DAMIEN ABOUT 3:30, AND YOU WERE ONLY ON THE PHONE WITH DAMIEN ABOUT 5 MINUTES THAT DAY, IS THAT RIGHT?

HOLLY: UM UM (YES)

RIDGE: UH, WHEN'S THE NEXT TIME AFTER THE PHONE CALLS THAT YOU SAW DAMIEN AGAIN?

HOLLY: LATE THAT FRIDAY NIGHT

This timeframe is also contradicted by an eye witness Carrie Morris who seen Damien on that day about 3:30-4:00 PM

STATEMENT OF: Carrie Morris
***Hokiday Drive
DOB: **-**-** S/R **/W/**

DATE: 9-29-93

On Wednesday, May 5, 1993, I was going toward Barton we, when I saw Michael Moore walking about 3 house's in front of Mr. Echols. Michael Moore was going home to get his bicycle to go trail riding with Steve Branch. This was at about 3:30 or 4p.m. About an hour later Michael, Steve, Chris came and ask my daughter (Tiffany Morris 8 years old) to go ridin with them. I told them no. We left to go to Memphis, when they were chasing my truck. This was about 4:30pm.

Damien & Michael were both walking South on 700 block North Wilson on the East side of the street. I know it was Damien Echols because I saw his picture in paper after he was arrested. I knew it was Michael from school and knowing his parents all my life & known Michael for about 3 years ever since they moved back from Florida.

CAM

3:45 P.M., on the 29 day of Sept. 1993

Doc# 003413

Carrie was given a lie detector test to follow up with her statement. She passed the test with no signs of deception.

#1 indicates where Damien was seen around 3:30-4:00 PM on the day the children came up missing. #2 shows the location that the bodies were found.

DAMIEN STATED THAT ON THURSDAY HE WENT TO LAKESHORE WHERE HE STATED WITH DOMINI. HE STATED THAT HE HEARD THE BOYS WERE MISSING FROM JASON BALDWIN WHILE HE WAS A LAKESHORE THAT DAY. HE THEN STATED THAT HE HEARD THAT THE NEWS THAT THE BOYS WERE MISSING FROM JASON'S MOTHER.

DAMIEN STATED THAT STEVE JONES FROM THE JUVENILE AUTHORITY HAD BEEN BY TO SEE HIM A DAY OR TWO BEFORE AND THAT STEVE HAD TOLD HIM ABOUT HOW THE BOYS TESTICLES HAD BEEN CUT OFF AND THAT SOMEONE HAD URINATED IN THEIR MOUTHS. HE STATED THAT STEVE STATED THAT COULD HAVE BEEN THE REASON THAT THE BODIES WERE PLACED IN THE

WATER SO THAT THE URINE COULD HAVE BEEN WASHED OUT.

DAMIEN HAD AN OPINION FOR WHO COULD HAVE DONE THE MURDERS AS BEING SOMEONE SICK AND THAT IT WAS SOME TYPE OF THRILL KILL. HE ALS STATED THAT THE PENIS WAS A SYMBOL OF POWER IN HIS RELIGION KNOWN AS WICCA. HE ALSO STATED THAT THE NUMBER 3 WAS A SACRED NUMBER IN THE BELIEF.

WHEN ASKED ABOUT JASON BALDWIN HE DESCRIBED A JASON BALDWIN THAT LIVED IN WEST THAT WAS NOT HIS FRIEND JASON BALDWIN. HE CLAIMED THAT THE OTHER WAS MEAN AND THAT HE HAD BEEN KNOWN TO KILL SNAKES WHICH HE CLAIMED WAS JUST FOR THE "HELL" OF KILLING. THIS JASON WAS DESCRIBED AS BEING ABOUT 5'9" TALL, 18 YEARS OLD, AND 300 POUNDS. HE STATED THAT HE THOUGHT JASON WAS KNOWN TO

SMOKE DOPE BUT, HE WAS NOT QUEER.

DAMIEN STATED THAT HE KNEW L.G. HOLLINGSWORTH THROUGH DOMINI. HE THOUGHT THAT L.G. WAS A RELATIVE BY MARRIAGE. HE STATED THAT L.G. WAS KIND OF WEIRD IN THAT ON ONE OCCASION HE WANTED TO TRADE GIRL FRIENDS WITH DAMIEN FOR A NIGHT.

WHEN ASKED ABOUT WHAT HE HAD HEARD ABOUT HOW THE MURDERS HAD OCCURRED HE STATED THAT THEY PROBABLY DIED OF MUTILATION. HE STATED THAT HE HEARD THAT SOME GUY HAD CUT THEM UP. HE HEARD THAT THEY WERE PLACED IN THE WATER AND THAT THEY MAY HAVE DROWNED. HE STATED THAT BECAUSE OF WHAT HE HAD HEARD HE BELIEVED THAT AT LEAST ONE OF THE BOYS HAD BEEN CUT UP. HE STATED THAT ONE OF THE BOYS MAY HAVE BEEN CUT

MORE THAN THE OTHERS. DAMIEN FELT THAT THE HOMICIDE MAY HAVE BEEN FOR THE PURPOSE OF TRYING TO SCARE SOMEONE.

DAMIEN STATED THAT HE FELT THAT IT WS PROBABLY ONE PERSON BECAUSE IF IT WERE MORE THAN ONE PERSON SOMEBODY WOULD PROBABLY TELL ABOUT IT SOONER OR LATER. HE SAID THAT THERE WOULD BE A FEAR OF SQUEALING BY ONE OF THE PERSON IN THE ACT IF IT WERE MORE THAN ONE PERSON.

WHEN ASKED IF THE WATER HAD ANY TYPE OF MEANING IN THE WICCA OR BLACK MAGIC, DAMIEN STATED THAT WATER WAS A DEMON TYPE SYMBOLISM AND THAT ALL PEOPLE HAVE A DEMONIC FORCE. HE FURTHER STATED THAT PEOPLE HAVE CONTROL OVER THE DEMONIC FORCE IN THEM.

WHEN ASKED ABOUT HOW HE THOUGHT THE PERSON FELT THAT

HAD DONE THE HOMICIDES, HE STATED THAT THE PERSON PROBABLY FELT GOOD ABOUT WHAT HE HAD DONE AND THAT HE FELT GOOD THAT HE HAD THE POWER TO DO WHAT HE HAD DONE.

WHEN ASKED WHY HE THOUGHT THE VICTIMS WERE SO YOUNG, HE STATED THAT THE YOUNGER THE VICTIM THEN THE MORE INNOCENT THE VICTIM WOULD BE. THAT IN TURN MEANT THAT THE MORE INNOCENT THE VICTIM WOULD BE THE MORE POWER THAT THE PERSON WOULD HAVE GOTTEN FROM THE SACRIFICE.

DAMIEN WENT FURTHER TO EXPLAIN THAT IN HIS WICCA RELIGION HE KNEW THAT EVIL DONE COMES BACK THREE TIMES. HE STATED THAT MEANT THAT ANY EVIL DONE BY A PERSON WOULD BE REWARDED BY THE PERSON DOING THE DEED HAVING THREE TIMES THE EVIL DONE TO HIM IN REVENGE.

DAMIEN STATED THAT HIS
FAVORITE BOOK OF THE BIBLE WAS
THAT OF REVELATIONS BECAUSE OF
THE STORIES IN IT ABOUT WHAT
WAS BEING DONE BY THE DEVIL
AND THE SUFFERING DONE BY
PEOPLE AT THE HANDS OF THE
DEVIL.

DAMIEN STATED THAT HE FIGURED
THAT THE KILLER KNEW THE KIDS
WENT INTO THE WOODS AND EVEN
ASKED THEM TO COME OUT TO THE
WOODS. HE STATED THAT THE BOYS
WERE NOT BIG, NOT SMART, AND
THEY WOULD HAVE BEEN EASY TO
CONTROL. HE ALSO FELT THE
KILLER WOULD NOT HAVE BEEN
WORRIED ABOUT THE BOYS
SCREAMING DUE TO IT BEING IN THE
WOODS AND CLOSE TO THE
EXPRESSWAY. HE FURTHER STATED
THAT THE KILLER PROBABLY
WANTED TO HEAR THE SCREAMING.

DAMIEN MENTIONED THAT HE
THOUGHT THAT IT WAS SCARY THAT

WE WERE DOING PSYCHOLOGICAL
PROFILES AND THAT HE WAS ON AN
ANTIDEPRESSANT THAT HE SAID
WAS AMIPROMIN.

WHEN ASKED WHAT HE THOUGHT
THE PERSON WHO KILLED THE BOYS
WAS FEELING NOW, DAMIEN STATED
THAT THE PERSON PROBABLY
THOUGHT IT WAS FUNNY AND THAT
HE DIDN'T CARE WHETHER OR NOT
HE GOT CAUGHT.

WHEN ASKED WHAT KINDS OF ITEMS
WE SHOULD BE SEARCHING FOR, HE
STATED THAT WE SHOULD BE
LOOKING FOR STONES IN THE AREA,
CANDLES, A KNIFE, AND SOME TYPE
OF CRYSTALS.

NOTE

At this point it is Damien who is suggesting that the WMPD look for evidence of cult activity

DAMIEN WAS ASKED WHAT KIND OF CIGARETTES HE WAS SMOKING AND HE STATED THAT HE SMOKED THE CHEAPEST BRAND THAT HE COULD FIND.

DAMIEN STATED THAT HE FELT THE MURDERER WOULD BE SOMEONE LOCAL AND THAT THE PERSON WOULD NOT FLEE FROM THE AREA.

DAMIEN WAS ASKED ABOUT HIS SEX LIFE AND HE STATED THAT HE NOW THOUGHT SEX WAS BORING.

IT WAS NOTED THAT DAMIEN HAD THE TATOO OF "E", "V", "I", AND "L" ACROSS HIS LEFT KNUCKLES AND HE STATED THAT JASON BALDWIN HAD THE SAME TATOO ON HIS KNUCKLES.

AT THIS TIME DAMIEN WAS ASKED IF HE WOULD SUBMIT TO HAVING HAIR SAMPLES TAKEN AND BLOOD SAMPLES. HE STATED THAT HE DID NOT OBJECT TO THE SAMPLES BEING TAKEN. IT WAS FURTHER ASKED IF HE WOULD BE WILLING TO TAKE A

POLYGRAPH EXAMINATION IF ONE COULD BE SCHEDULED AND HE AGAIN STATED THAT HE WOULD TAKE THE TEST.

LT. SUDBURY THEN LEFT THE ROOM AND ATTEMPTED TO SET UP A POLYGRAPH EXAMINATION TO DETERMINE IF HE WAS BEING TRUTHFUL IN HIS STATEMENTS. I ASKED DAMIEN IF HE CONSIDERED HIMSELF TO BE INTELLIGENT AT WHICH TIME HE STATED THAT HE THOUGHT HE WAS VERY INTELLIGENT. HE STATED THAT HE DROPPED OUT OF SCHOOL BUT THAT HE WAS SELF TAUGHT AND THAT HE WAS VERY SMART AND MORE INTELLIGENT THAN MOST PEOPLE.

LT. SUDBURY HAD ASKED QUESTIONS THROUGHOUT THE INTERVIEW THAT HE HAD LISTED. LT. SUDBURY KEPT NOTES HIMSELF AS TO THE ANSWERS THAT DAMIEN HAD GIVEN TO HIS QUESTIONS.

Damien's Polygraph Test

AT THIS TIME DAMIEN WAS TURNED OVER TO DETECTIVE DURHAM FOR A POLYGRAPH EXAMINATION.

AFTER A TIME DETECTIVE DURHAM CAME AND MET WITH ME AND OTHER OFFICERS AND REPORTED THAT DAMIEN HAD BEEN UNTRUTHFUL AND ACCORDING TO THE POLYGRAPH WAS INVOLVED IN THE MURDERS. IT WAS DETERMINED AT THIS TIME DETECTIVE DURHAM AND LT. SUDBURY WOULD CONTINUE THE INTERROGATION THAT HAD BEGUN WHEN IT WAS DISCOVERED THAT HE WAS BEING UNTRUTHFUL.

Polygraph Test and Report for Damien Echols (West Memphis Police, May 10, 1993)

These are the ten questions that investigators asked Damien during the testing process.

IN 1. HAVE YOU EVER TAKEN A POLYGRAPH TEST BEFORE?

SR 2. IN REGARD TO THE MURDER OF THOSE THREE YOUNG BOYS, ARE YOU GOING TO TELL THE TRUTH DURING THIS TEST?

R 3. AT ANY TIME WEDNESDAY OR WEDNESDAY NIGHT, WERE YOU IN ROBIN HOOD HILLS?

C. 4. HAVE YOU EVER KILLED A CAT OR A DOG?

R. 5. WERE YOU PRESENT WHEN THOSE BOYS WERE KILLED?

C 6. HAVE YOU EVER TAKEN PART IN DEVIL WORSHIP?

R. 7. DID YOU KILL ANY OF THOSE THREE BOYS?

IN 8. HAVE YOU TAKEN ANY DRUGS OR MEDICATION TODAY?

R. 9. DO YOU KNOW WHO KILLED THOSE THREE BOYS?

10. DO YOU SUSPECT ANYONE OF HAVING KILLED THOSE THREE BOYS?

POLYGRAPH REPORT
(May 10, 1993)

Polygraph chart for Echols, showing responses to questions 6 - 10.

TO: DET. RIDGE DATE OF EXAM MAY 10, 1993

COMPLAINANT NUMBER CASE FILE NUMBER 93-05-0666

SUBJECT DAMIEN WAYNE ECHOLS

ADDRESS 2706 SOUTH GROVE DLN.

CITY/STATE WEST MEMPHIS, AR. D.O.B. 12-11-74

PURPOSE OF EXAMINATION: HOMICIDE INVESTIGATION

REMARKS:

IN THE PRETEST INTERVIEW, THE SUBJECT DENIED HAVING BEEN IN ROBIN HOOD HILLS ON WEDNESDAY, MAY 5, 1993. HE DENIED BEING PRESENT WHEN THE VICTIMS WERE KILLED AND DENIED HAVING KILLED ANY OF THE VICTIMS. HE ALSO SAID HE DID NOT KNOW WHO KILLED THE THREE VICTIMS.

A TEN QUESTION POLYGRAPH TEST WAS FORMULATED AND THREE POLYGRAPH CHARTS WERE CONDUCTED. THE TEST CONTAINED THE FOLLOWING RELEVANT QUESTIONS:

Q.#3. AT ANY TIME WEDNESDAY OR WEDNESDAY NIGHT, WERE YOU IN ROBIN HOOD HILLS? "NO"

Q.#5. WERE YOU PRESENT WHEN THOSE BOYS WERE KILLED? "NO"

Q.#7. DID YOU KILL ANY OF THOSE THREE BOYS? "NO"

Q.#9. DO YOU KNOW WHO KILLED THOSE THREE BOYS? "NO"

Q.#10.DO YOU SUSPECT ANYONE OF HAVING KILLED THOSE THREE BOYS? "NO"

IT IS THE OPINION OF THIS POLYGRAPH EXAMINER THAT THIS SUBJECT RECORDED SIGNIFICANT RESPONSES INDICATIVE OF DECEPTION WHEN HE ANSWERED THE ABOVE LISTED RELEVANT QUESTIONS IN THE MANNER NOTED.

CONCLUSION: DECEPTION INDICATED

IN THE POST TEST INTERVIEW, THE SUBJECT DENIED ANY INVOLVEMENT IN THIS CRIME.

AFTER APPROXIMATELY FORTY-FIVE MINUTES, I ASKED THE SUBJECT WHAT WAS HE AFRAID OF? HE REPLIED: "THE ELECTRIC CHAIR". HE THEN SAID THAT HE LIKED THE HOSPITAL IN LITTLE ROCK. (HE SAID HE HAD BEEN TREATED THERE FOR MANIC-DEPRESSION) AFTER A SHORT PERIOD OF TIME, THE SUBJECT CEASED TO DENIE HIS INVOLVEMENT. (ADMISSION THROUGH ABSENCE OF DENIAL) HE THEN SAID: "I WILL TELL YOU ALL ABOUT IT IF YOU WILL LET ME TALK TO MY MOTHER." DETECTIVE RIDGE BROUGHT HIS MOTHER IN TO MY OFFICE TO TALK TO HIM. AFTER TALKING TO HIS MOTHER HE AGAIN DENIED BEING INVOLVED IN THE MURDERS. AFTER APPROXIMATELY TWENTY MINUTES, I ASKED: "YOUR'E NEVER GOING TO TELL ANYONE ABOUT THIS BUT YOUR DOCTOR, ARE YOU?" HE REPLIED: "NO".

Bill Durham

The results of Damien's failed lie detector test and the fact that he lied about his whereabouts on the day of the murders was not released to the general public. Some of the people that had been interviewed for the writing of this book were never aware of the conflicting statements to Damien's alibi or the fact that he failed the lie detector test. Most of the people that we spoke to admitted that they based their opinions on the case solely by what they had read in the newspapers or heard on television.

When we sat down and showed them the reports that we discovered they all had a change of heart as to their personal belief that Damien Echols was innocent.

We would also like to point out that at no time during any of the statements made by Damien does he ever state that Jessie Misskelley was with him on the day that the murders occurred.

CHAPTER FOUR

CONFESSIONS AND CONFUSION

JESSIE MISSKELLEY

As you read the information found in this chapter we will be pointing out the discrepancies in Jessie's statement to police. We will also add in information that was presented at trial to support the facts of these discrepancies. The purpose of this is to give you the reader the facts surrounding Jessie Misskelley and his so called confession, right from the start. Some of this information will be repeated in further chapters.

We will also like to note that the reports and statements in this book came from public records and court documents. They are here exactly as they are written. We did not correct any typos or errors. This was done to keep the integrity of the facts.

The grotesque nature of the murders led to a theory about satanic cult activity. Investigators focused their attention on Damien Echols who at the time was a troubled, yet gifted teenager who practiced Wicca, a rarity in the town of West Memphis. Efforts to learn more about him, spearheaded by a single mother cooperating with the police, led to Mr. Misskelley, who at the time was a passing acquaintance of Echols.

Certain that they had their prime suspect, police would focus their investigation toward looking for evidence which would enable them to arrest Damien Echols. Any known associates of Damien were also questioned. Both Damien and his close friend Jason Baldwin received many visits from police who would often park near their homes at night in the hope that such intimidation would break them.

On 6 May 1993, the day the bodies were discovered, WMPD received a call from Don Bray at the Marion County Police Department to inform them that a young boy was there who claimed to know something about the murders. Aaron Hutcheson had been at the police department with his mother Vicky Hutcheson when he had told Bray that the boys had been "at the playhouse." WMPD officers told Bray that the location was near where the boys were found. However, no playhouse was found when the police took Aaron to the crime scene. Later, Aaron claimed that he had actually witnessed the murders. His first claim was that he had seen men in the woods dressed up and speaking "Spanish", then later he said that he had seen John Mark Byers kill the boys.

Despite the obvious inconsistencies in the boy's many stories, police attempted to get him to identify Jason and Damien in a photo line-up but he was unable to do so. He did not actually identify any of the three until after Jessie's confession to police in June. Jessie often babysat for Aaron and knew him well.

Eventually the prosecution decided not to use Aaron's testimony because his story changed so much. And people who knew Aaron placed him well away from the crime scene at the time of the murders. Despite this, the media quickly learned that the police had a witness to the crimes, severely prejudicing the case.

In June 2014 we were able to talk to a reporter from the local news media who reported on the case back in 1993. She told us that from the very beginning this story was considered a page one column. And that their job was to sell papers and if it meant that they had to sensationalize the story then that was what they did. She said that they would meet daily to discuss the story and evidence prior to printing anything in the paper. And the only thing that the editors and publisher wanted was what was going to keep the paper sales numbers up, not particularly the truth.

She said, "When the public was calling it a cult killing so did we. We knew from the very beginning that this was not a cult killing but if we printed that then no one would buy our papers."

We asked her what she thought about the guilt or innocence of the three boys arrested. She told us, "Out of the three boys arrested, all of the reporters on the case felt that Jessie was the only innocent one in the group. We had been told from day one not to report any information that would make any of the three look innocent."

A former editor for one of the local newspapers said, "After the trial we learned about some evidence that was never released to the public or even used in the trial. We decided not to bring this information out basically we decided to keep it out of the public's eye. We did this because now the focus was turned to the idea that these guys were in fact innocent. And if we wanted to sell papers we had to print what the people wanted to hear."

Vicki was disappointed that she would no longer be receiving any reward for Aaron's assistance to the police; she then agreed to let the police wire her house in an attempt to tape Damien talking about the murders. She did not know Damien personally so she asked Jessie to arrange for Damien to come to her home. Although Jessie claims he did not know Damien, he was able to arrange for Damien to meet with Vicki just prior to his arrest. The entire conversation was taped but no information helpful to the police was recorded. Police claim that there was nothing audible on the tape at all, although Vicki later claimed she had heard the tape at

WMPD and everything could be heard clearly.

The next day, Vicki Hutcheson made a statement to police; she said that two weeks after the murders she had gone with Jessie and Damien to an Esbat (a ritual observance of the full moon within Wicca and other Wiccan-influenced forms of Neopaganism) in Turrell, AR. She claimed that Damien had driven his red Ford Escort to the empty field where the Esbat supposedly occurred. Although Damien Echols did not have a driver's license and did not own or have access to a Ford Escort, and Vicki was not able to identify anyone else attending the Esbat or even find its location, Vicki Hutcheson was still used during the trial as a corroborative witness to Damien and Jessie's Satanic involvements. Years later after the trials were over; Vicki admitted that she had made up the story. In later court proceedings she was not allowed to actually testify in open court about her false testimony, because the prosecutors threatened her with charges of perjury. This would of put the states original case and convictions in jeopardy.

The police became even more convinced of Jessie's involvement when William Winfred Jones told them that Damien, while drunk, had bragged to him about murdering the boys. Before he could testify in Jessie's trial, however, Jones recanted his statement, telling police that he had in fact lied about these events; he had only heard rumors of Damien's involvement. Both of these witnesses' statements led police to Jessie Misskelley for questioning. It seems that the offer of a reward for assisting police in arresting the killers was too much for some people to resist.

Two of the leading factors that destroyed this case were the fact that people were making up stories to try to get the reward money. One former West Memphis police officer said, "Everyone who made any claims that they knew anything about the case was just telling us what the papers and news stations were already saying." Unfortunately the West Memphis Police were more focused on making an arrest then solving the case. Even a first year rookie police officer could see the problems with this investigation.

The police had another person to talk to, Jessie Misskelley. After the trial and convictions the major witch hunt theory on this case was centered on the day that Jessie was questioned and eventually confessed to his part in the crime.

The information regarding this day has been so spun out of shape that all of the lies have become fact in the eyes of the supporters for the West Memphis three. One of the biggest misconceptions was that Jessie was questioned for over 12 hours prior to his statement being recorded. This in fact was not true.

The actual interview started about 10:00 am and the recorded statement was taken at 2:44 pm and ended at 3:18 pm. (the interview prior to the recorded statement lasted a total of 4 hours and 44 minutes, not 12 hours)

Jessie Misskelley was brought in to WMPD for questioning on June 3rd, 1993 at around 10:00 am. During the course of his interrogation, which lasted for almost five hours, Jessie was given a lie detector test and the police succeeded in securing a confession from Jessie of his own part in the murders of the three boys. He named Jason Baldwin and Damien Echols as his accomplices.

Jessie's confession did not match with significant details with the facts of the crime known by the police. Most experienced law enforcement investigators would question the validity of this confession. But the West Memphis Police were so fixated on making an arrest that they overlooked basic police training and fixated on the witch hunt mentality.

Jessie was also questioned despite the fact that they did not have a written waiver of his Miranda Rights signed by Jessie's father, a legal requirement when police interview minors. The WM3 supporters focused that not only was Jessie a minor being only 17 at the time of his arrest but his mental capacity was well below that of normal 17 year olds with an IQ of only 72. But just like numerous other statements made by the supporters of the WM3 this was also not factual.

There have been numerous issues with the WM3 supporters on the fact of Jessie's IQ. Some have falsely reported that Jessie was mentally retarded. And this false information spearheaded a lot of debates on the significance of Jessie's confession.

We will take this opportunity to state that Jessie Misskelley is not mentally retarded.

 Not by any accepted legal or medical definition, at least. No one disputes that he has a low IQ, but that is not synonymous with "mentally retarded".
The bogus "mentally retarded" claim serves two purposes for WM3 supporters: creating sympathy ("look at how the mean cops

treated poor retarded Jessie") and casting doubt about Jessie's many confessions ("you can't believe anything Jessie says, he's mentally retarded").

Misskelley's lawyers even tried to depict him as "mentally retarded" during trial. Supporters continue to call him "mentally retarded", or "mildly retarded" or "borderline retarded" or "mentally handicapped".

But this is not true. Misskelley's lawyer and WM3 defenders often make the similar claim that Misskelley functions at a five-year-old level. Again, there's no evidence for this claim. He was 17 at the time of the crime and confession, and he functioned at the level of a street-smart but low-IQ 17-year-old.

In the fall of 1993, when Misskelley was awaiting trial, a psychologist hired by Misskelley's defense lawyers gave him an IQ test (specifically, the WAIS-R). Dr. William Wilkins declared Misskelley's IQ to be 72. Before the murders, Misskelley had taken two other IQ tests and scored 74 and 73.

But the jailhouse IQ test should be taken with a grain of salt. First, Misskelley's lawyer told him upfront that a lower test score would make the death penalty less likely. *Paradise Lost* actually shows this conversation (around the 13:00 mark). That's a pretty strong incentive to get a few questions wrong.

Second, cross-examination of Dr. Wilkins brought out some very important discrepancies. In Misskelley's two earlier IQ tests, his performance score (a sub-score covering five of the eleven subtests in the WAIS-R) had been 84 and 88; this time around his performance score was 75. The prosecutor also grilled Wilkins about The Minnesota Multiphasic Personality Inventory (MMPI-2 test) which is a personality test, not an IQ test given to Misskelley, which showed a very high level of "malingering" or "faking bad" or, in Wilkins' own words, "trying to present yourself as being ill when you're not for some particular gain". Wilkins falsely reported a "mild elevation" on the malingering scale in his report; under cross-examination he admitted, *"That may have been a mistake then. I may well have mispronounced what it was supposed to be."* All very technical, but the upshot is: Misskelley may have intentionally tried to score badly on his psychological tests, and Dr. Wilkins may have been complicit in this attempt.

That IQ score of 72 should not be taken as hard fact. Consider it the low end of a range. And even a score of 72 does not mean someone is mentally retarded.

Here is a rough breakdown of mental retardation
Profound mental retardation: Below 20
Severe mental retardation: 20–34
Moderate mental retardation: 35–49
Mild mental retardation: 50–69
Misskelley definitely falls on the non-retarded side of the scale on all these "adaptive functioning" criteria. He lived very independently, going to jobs and

hanging with friends with little adult oversight. He juggled multiple relationships with women. Watch Jessie interact with his family in *Paradise Lost* — he holds up his end of the conversation, uses humor, responds quickly to things other people say. There's a broad range between "average intelligence" and "mentally retarded". I believe that Jessie Misskelley's cognitive level falls somewhere in the middle of that broad range.

Supporters of the West Memphis 3 have created so many false statements about Jessie Misskelley's 6/3/93 confession that it is almost impossible to decipher the facts from fiction. Some of the more popular false information that was spread was the following:

The police bullied a mentally retarded teenager into making a false confession in a brutal 12-hour interrogation;

We already covered the time line of the events on the day that Jessie was questioned and the facts surrounding his IQ. Both parts of this statement are proven to be false.

Jessie's family didn't know where he was;

Jessie Misskelley's father knew that his son was at the police station. Jessie Sr. talked to Sgt. Mike Allen at 9:45 am and again at 11:15 am about the interview. Allen actually talked to Jessie Sr. first in the morning prior to speaking with Jessie Jr.; Jessie Sr. then drove off and retrieved Jessie Jr.; then Allen and Jessie Jr. drove to the police station. At the 11:15 am meeting, Jessie Sr. signed a waiver allowing police to give Jessie Jr. a polygraph exam.

The supporters of the WM3 wanted to portray that Jessie's interview was a covert operation and that Jessie's father had no knowledge of it even happening. Unfortunately, there is documentation that shows that this statement made by the supporters of the WM3 is indeed false.

Rumors were also spread that Jessie was denied access to a lawyer, and that he was never informed of his Miranda rights. Some have even gone to the extreme of saying that Jessie was pressured into signing a rights waiver which he couldn't read or understand;

In fact the West Memphis Police informed Misskelley of his legal rights on several occasions. Sgt. Allen read Misskelley his legal rights around 11 am, and Misskelley initialed and signed a rights form. Detective Durham advised Misskelley of his rights again at around 11:30 am before conducting the polygraph exam, and Misskelley again initialed and signed a rights form. (This second form is not available online, but it was discussed and entered into evidence as "States Exhibit Eleven" during a court hearing on 1/13/94.)

At the beginning of the first tape-recorded confession, police again reminded Misskelley of his legal rights and reviewed the signed rights form with him. At that time

Jessie agreed to continue without a lawyer being present.

That hasn't stopped WM3 supporters from making bogus claims. For example, Henry Rollins told a radio interviewer in 2003, *"what was really interesting to me was the lack of due process that the three boys incarcerated did not enjoy and the lack of Miranda rights read to Jessie Misskelley and I went 'wow, that's not the way Americans should be treated'"*.

Had the facts been actually reviewed and not created in the minds of so many people, then it would have been common knowledge that Jessie Misskelley was not denied his rights to have a lawyer present during questioning.

Jessie Misskelley was capable of understanding his legal rights. His lawyers tried claiming that Misskelley was incapable of reading or understanding his legal rights, and because of that his confession should be thrown out. Prosecutors showed that Misskelley had extensive experience dealing with law enforcement officials before June 1993, and that Misskelley had been Mirandized and signed legal rights waivers on four previous occasions. It is my personal belief that with Jessie's criminal past and his mentality that he did in fact understand the Miranda Rights that were read to him by Sgt. Allen.

On numerous occasions some of the WM3 supporters claimed that Jessie was beaten and threatened during the interview process.

There's no evidence that Jessie Misskelley was threatened or harmed during his interrogation. Jessie Sr. later told reporters that cops "cussed him, spit in his face, stepped on his hands." It is possible officers used swear words around Jessie, but there's no evidence of any physical intimidation.

I do believe that Jessie Misskelley's story didn't match the facts of the crime, except for a few details which the cops fed him and had him repeat back. There are too many inconsistencies with the facts of this case and the statement made by Jessie.

We spoke to a former West Memphis police officer that was working at the time of the murders. He told us, "A lot of us didn't believe that Jessie was involved with this murder. His story did not add up and we knew that the detectives were leading him into what to say. But we had our hands tied because it would have been a career ending move to speak up and say anything." When we asked him why the detectives would have made the decision to coerce a confession out of Jessie his reply was, "We knew without a shadow of a doubt that Echols was involved and later we had reason to believe that Baldwin was involved also. Too many things did not add up with those two. But the detectives did not have anything solid to justify an arrest warrant. I believe that the detectives were so set on making the arrests that they used Jessie to do that."

According to Jessie's defense attorney, Daniel Stidham, Jessie claims that he and his friends were first approached by the police and offered a reward for information about the murders. Some people question why Jessie did not come forward then if he did in fact have information to give to the police.

Dan Stidham

In his confession, Jessie claimed that Jason telephoned him very early on the morning of the 5th of May. During this conversation, Jason had asked Jessie to accompany him and Damien to the Robin Hood Hills area. At first, Jessie stated that he had gone to the

Robin Hood area at about 9:00 a.m. that day to an area near a creek where he met up with Damien and Jason. He said that they were actually in the creek when the three boys rode up on their bicycles. Baldwin and Echols had called to the boys who then came to the creek. Jessie said that Baldwin and Echols began to severely beat the boys. Jessie, who was claiming to be merely an observer, said that at least two of the boys were raped and forced to perform oral sex on Baldwin and Echols. While these events were occurring, (James) Michael Moore had attempted to escape by running away, but Jessie had caught him and returned him to Baldwin and Echols.

Jessie stated that Jason had used a knife to cut the boys' faces and the penis area of Christopher Byers. He also stated that Echols had used a large stick to hit one of the boys and to strangle one of them. After the attack the boys' clothes were removed and they were tied up, Jessie said that he then left the scene. He was sure that Christopher Byers was already dead. After Jessie arrived home, he claimed that he was telephoned by Jason who apparently said "We done it!" And "What are we going to do if somebody saw us?" Jessie also said that he could hear Damien in the background.

When Jessie was asked whether he had ever been involved in a cult, he said that he had been for about three months. He told police that they usually met in the woods where they engaged in orgies and initiation rites which included killing and eating dogs. He stated that at one of these meetings, he saw a photograph that Echols had taken of the three boys and claimed that Echols had been watching the boys.

Jessie was asked to describe what Baldwin and Echols were wearing at the time of the murders. He told police that Jason had been wearing blue jeans, black lace-up boots and a T-shirt with a skull and the name of the band "Metallica" on it. Damien was wearing black pants, boots and a black T-shirt.

During the course of this first statement, Jessie changed the time that the murders occurred from 9:00 a.m. to 12:00 p.m. and explained that the three boys had skipped school. These times were again changed in another recorded statement taken two hours after the first one had concluded. In this statement Jessie said that he, Baldwin and Echols had arrived at the Robin Hood area between 5:00 p.m. and 6:00 p.m., but after prompting from one of the interviewing officers, he again changed this time to between 7:00 p.m. and 8:00 p.m. The final time Jessie gave was that the teenagers had arrived at 6:00 p.m. and the victims had arrived when it was nearly dark.

This misinformation on the time frame from Jessie should have thrown up multiple red flags that Jessie was in fact making up the story about what had happened on that day.

In his second statement, Jessie gave further details about the sexual molestation of the boys. He stated that the boys had been held by the head and ears and forced to perform oral sex on Jason and Damien. He named Steven Branch and Christopher Byers as the two victims who were raped. He stated that the boys had been tied with brown rope. It was a known fact to the investigators that the boys were not tied with rope but with their own shoe laces. And the chances that Jessie would mistake shoe laces for brown rope was very unlikely.

A further contradiction in Jessie's story was added later when one of the interrogating officers testified in court that according to his notes, Jessie had claimed that Baldwin had called him the night before the murders had occurred and said that they planned to go and get some boys and hurt them. When we look at that statement in light if everything else, we can only assume that this was also a lie. There would have been no way that Baldwin would know "the night prior" to the murders that the boys would be in the Robin Hood hills area the following day, let alone the exact time that they would be there also.

Jessie's lawyer Dan Stidham was able to secure the expert testimonies of Dr. Richard Ofshe and Warren Homes. Dr. Ofshe, a Pulitzer Prize winning social psychologist and an expert on false and coerced confessions, believed after reading the confession, listening to the tape and interviewing Jessie Misskelley, that Jessie's confession was a coerced compliant and false confession. The reasons given for this conclusion were:

1. Many instances of coaching from the interrogating officers, especially in regard to the timing of events and Jessie's identification of Christopher Byers as the boy who had been emasculated.

2. That nearly three hours of the interview was not recorded.

3. That the interrogating officers had used intimidating methods during the interrogation.

4. That many areas of Jessie's confession were not supported by the facts.

Some more incorrect information in Jessie's "confession:"

1. Jessie stated that the victims and Jason Baldwin were not at school when in fact

they were proven to have been in attendance

2. Jessie stated that the victims were bound with rope when in fact they were bound with their own shoelaces

3. Jessie stated that one boy was choked with a stick when the medical examiner's report stated that there was no evidence of strangulation

4. Jessie stated that the boys were anally raped when in fact the medical examiner had found no evidence of this occurring

5. Jessie described the murders as having been committed at the scene where the bodies were found when in fact the medical examiner had stated that there was no blood found at the scene.

Dr. Ofshe was not permitted to state all of his opinion during the trial as Judge Burnett had previously ruled that Jessie's confession had been voluntary and Ofshe's testimony in this regard would directly contradict the court's previous ruling. Burnett also stated that such a testimony would give an expert witness the power to determine whether the accused was guilty or innocent which was solely the jury's domain. Finally, the jury only heard that Ofshe had a lot of experience with coerced confessions and it was possible for police to obtain a confession from someone who was in fact innocent. Anything more specific was not allowed.

Many lawyers who have reviewed the case and all of the evidence believe that Jessie was in fact coerced into making his confession to "somewhat" fit the crime. It is also believed that had all the facts about the confession been revealed in Jessie's trial that he would have been found innocent by the jury.

Unfortunately the confession was not as much to convict Jessie as it was to give justification for an arrest warrant for Damien Echols and Jason Baldwin.

Warren Holmes, an expert in lie detection testing and interrogation procedures who has studied and worked in this field for over 30 years, agreed to testify for the defense after he was approached by Daniel Stidham, despite the knowledge that he would not be paid for his services and only his expenses would be reimbursed.

At a hearing prior to the trial, Judge Burnett ruled that Warren Holmes could not testify regarding the polygraph examination itself. As polygraph test results are not admissible evidence he would only allow Holmes to testify to his experience and qualifications and to give an analyses of the interview techniques used during Jessie Misskelley's interrogation.

When Holmes analyzed the polygraph test conducted by the WMPD on Jessie Misskelley he found that Jessie's responses to the questions relating to the murders indicated that Jessie was truthful in his answers and in fact did not have any knowledge of them. The WMPD interrogating officers' statement to Jessie that he had in fact been untruthful indicated to Holmes that they had not conducted or interpreted the results of the tests properly. The result of Jessie being informed that he was lying would have greatly contributed to Jessie's sense of helplessness in the situation making him more likely to comply with the demand for a confession by the police.

According to Holmes there are a number of indicators which will validate to the investigators that a suspect's confession is true.

1. In a true confession, the suspect will often give the police information about the crime that the police do not already know.

2. If a confession is true, the suspect gives information that fits with the real evidence of the crime.

3. A true confession is usually given in a narrative form including many incidental details about the situation surrounding the crime which can be corroborated by police later

4. In a true confession, if the investigators make an incorrect supposition about the crime, the suspect will correct them.

5. In a true confession, there is no need to correct the suspect for contradictions in their story.

6. In a true confession, there is no need for coaching or leading questions in order to elicit information.

Homes believed that there were many instances in Jessie's confession where these criteria were not met. He was especially concerned that Jessie was wrong about the times and the type of ligatures used. Both of these factors should have meant a great deal to him. Jessie also did not mention anything about his feelings at the time of the crimes or afterwards, nor does he talk about the things that were said by either himself, the other perpetrators or the victims. Jessie's confession was elicited by a series of highly suggestive questions by the interrogating officers and was not given in a narrative form.

The testimony of these two witnesses was the strongest evidence that the defense had to refute the prosecution's case which was built solely upon the weight of Jessie's confession. Without this expert opinion, Jessie's case was severely hampered.

Here is a detailed time frame of the events of June 3rd 1993. This information was obtained from The West Memphis Police Department's official records of events.

#006048-

8:00 AM SQUAD MEETING/DISCUSSED ATTEMPTING TO PICK UP JESSIE MISSKELLEY JR IN REFERENCE TO HIS BEING A MEMBER OF CULT THAT DAMIEN ECHOLS AND JASON BALDWIN ARE SAID TO BE MEMBERS OF. CHECK POSSIBILITY OF HIS BEING A WITNESS TO HOMICIDE OR ANY STATEMENTS HE MAY HAVE OVERHEARD FROM DAMIEN OR ANYONE CONCERNING THE HOMICIDE.

9:13 AM DETECTIVE SGT. MIKE ALLEN CHECKED INTO SERVICE

DETECTIVE ALLEN WENT TO THE RESIDENCE OF JESSIE MISSKELLEY JR. TO ATTEMPT TO MAKE CONTACT. CONTACTED THE FEMALE WHO WAS AT THE RESIDENCE WHO INFORMED THAT JESSIE JR. WAS NOT AT THE RESIDENCE. SHE INFORMED ALLEN THAT HE COULD GO TO JIM'S DIESEL REPAIR AND MEET WITH JESSIE MISSKELLEY SR.

9:45 AM ALLEN WENT TO JIM'S REPAIR AND MET WITH JESSIE SR. WHO WENT AND PICKED UP JESSIE MISSKELLEY JR. JESSIE MISSKELLEY JR. THEN WENT WITH DETECTIVE ALLEN TO THE WEST MEMPHIS POLICE DEPARTMENT.

10:00 AM DETECTIVE SGT. ALLEN

FILLED OUT THE SUBJECT
DESCRIPTION FORM AND THE
INTERVIEW BEGAN WITH THE
QUESTIONS OR ANY KNOWLEDGE HE
HAD OF THE HOMICIDE AND HIS
WHEREABOUTS ON THE DAY OF THE
HOMICIDE.

11:00 AM DETECTIVE ALLEN READ
JESSIE MISSKELLEY JR. HIS RIGHTS
ACCORDING TO THE MIRANDA RULE
WITH DETECTIVE RIDGE BEING A
WITNESS TO THE PROCEDURE. IT
WAS DETERMINED THAT IT WOULD
BE NECESSARY FOR JESSIE
MISSKELLEY SR. TO SIGN A CONSENT
TO ALLOW JESSIE JR. TO SUBMIT TO
A POLYGRAPH EXAMINATION.

11:15 AM SGT. ALLEN WENT WITH
JESSIE MISSKELLEY JR. TO FIND HIS
FATHER TO OBTAIN A CONSENT TO
TAKE A POLYGRAPH EXAMINATION.

SGT. ALLEN HAD JESSIE RIDING AS A UNSECURED PASSENGER IN THE FRONT SEAT AT WHICH TIME HE MET JESSIE AT OR NEAR MISSOURI STREET AND SHOPPINGWAY. SGT. ALLEN MET WITH JESSIE MISSKELLEY SR. AT CHIEF'S AUTO PARTS WHERE HE EXPLAINED THE UPCOMING PROCEDURE AND OBTAINED A WRITTEN CONSENT FOR JESSIE MISSKELLEY TO TAKE A POLYGRAPH EXAMINATION.

11:30 AM JESSIE MISSKELLEY JR. WAS READ HIS RIGHTS ACCORDING TO THE MIRANDA RULE BY BILL DURHAM PRIOR TO HIS ADMINISTERING A POLYGRAPH EXAMINATION.

006047

11:55 AM FIRST CHART WAS

COMPLETED DURING POLYGRAPH EXAMINATION.

12:03 PM SECOND CHART COMPLETED DURING POLYGRAPH EXAMINATION

12:11 PM THIRD CHART COMPLETED DURING POLYGRAPH EXAMINATION. AFTER THE TEST ABOUT 15 MINUTES WERE SPENT IN THE POST TEST INTERVIEW.

12:30 PM BILL DURHAM ADVISED DETECTIVE RIDGE, INSPECTOR GITCHELL, AND SGT. MIKE ALLEN THAT JESSIE MISSKELLEY WAS BEING DECEPTIVE IN HIS RESPONSES TO THE RELEVANT QUESTIONS ASKED DURING THE POLYGRAPH EXAMINATION.

12:40 PM IT WAS DECIDED THAT

DETECTIVE RIDGE AND INSPECTOR GITCHELL WOULD CONTINUE THE INTERVIEW.

2:20 PM JESSIE STATES TO INSPECTOR GITCHELL THAT HE WAS PRESENT WHEN THE THREE BOYS WERE KILLED. PREPARATIONS WERE BEGUN TO TAPE THE REST OF THE INTERROGATION WHEN IT WAS DETERMINED THAT JESSIE WAS A DIRECT WITNESS OR A PARTICIPANT OF THE HOMICIDE.

2:44 PM THE TAPED CONFESSION BEGAN WITH JESSIE MISSKELLEY JR. BEING QUESTIONED BY DETECTIVE RIDGE AND INSPECTOR GITCHELL.

Here is the entire transcript of the interview with Jessie Misskelley on June 3rd 1993. We have added it word for word from the transcripts of the West Memphis Police Department's files. We did not change any typos in the report to keep the validity of the information.

Statement of Jessie L. Misskelley, Jr. 6/3/93

Date of Birth 7/10/7 5 sex/race M/Cau

RIDGE: This is Det. Bryn Ridge of the West Memphis Police Depart- ment, currently in the detective division of the West Memphis Police Department conducting an investigation of the Triple Homicide, Case File # 93-05-0666. Currently in the office with Jessie Lloyd Misskelly, Jr., DOB: 7/10/75, education: 9th grade, the place: Detective Division, todays date is 06/03/93, the time is 2:44Pm. Present in the interview is Insp. Gary Gitchell and Jessie Misskelly. Jessie, in front of me I have a rights form, and it has your signature at the bottom of it, is that your signature?
JESSIE: Yes sir
RIDGE: okay, we are informing you that we are Det. Sgt. Mike Allen, and Det. Bryn

Ridge, and Det. Sgt. Mike Allen is the one that read this form to you earlier, is that correct?

JESSIE: Yes sir

RIDGE: And I was here when he read it to you.

JESSIE: Yes sir

RIDGE: Alright, we are police officers of the West Memphis Police Department, we are conducting an investigation for the offense Capitol Felony Murder, which was committed on or about 05/05/93, before we ask you any questions, you must know and understand your legal rights, therefore, we warn and advise you, that you have the right to remain silent , do you understand that?

JESSIE: Yes

RIDGE: And those are your initials on the line in front of that statement?

JESSIE: Yes

RIDGE: Okay, anything you say can be used against you in court, do you understand that,

JESSIE: Yes, I do

RIDGE: And those are your initials?

JESSIE: Yes, it is

RIDGE: Alright, you have the right to talk to a lawyer for advise before we ask you any questions, and to have him with you during questioning, do you understand that?

JESSIE: Yes, I do

RIDGE: And those are your initals?

JESSIE: Yes, it is

RIDGE: If you cannot afford a lawyer, one will be appointed for you before any questions, if you wish, at no cost to you, do you understand that?

JESSIE: Yes, I do

RIDGE: And those are your initials?

JESSIE: Yes, it is

RIDGE: If you decide to answer questions now without a lawyer present you will still have the right to stop answering at any time, do you understand?

JESSIE: Yes, I do

RIDGE: Those are your initials?

JESSIE: Yes, it is

RIDGE: You're up here on your own free will, you came up here to answer some questions, and basically we've found out some information during that questioning, is that correct?

JESSIE: Yes sir, I did

RIDGE: Okay, at the bottom of the form is a Waiver of Rights, it says that I've read this statement of my rights, and I understand what my rights are, I am willing to make a statement, and answer questions, I do not want a lawyer at this time, I understand and know what I am doing. No promises or threats have been made to me, and no pressure or force has been used against me, is all of that correct?

JESSIE: Yes

RIDGE: Okay, and you signed the bottom of the form?

JESSIE: Yes, I did

RIDGE: Witnessed by Michael Wayne Allen and myself, Det. Bryn Ridge. Okay, Jessie, let's go straight to that date,

05/05/93, Wednesday, early in the morning. You received a phone call is that correct?

JESSIE: Yes, I did

RIDGE: And who made that phone call?

JESSIE: Jason Baldwin

RIDGE: Alright, what occurred, what did he talk about?

JESSIE: He called me and asked me if I could go to West Memphis with him and I told him, no, I had to work and stuff. He told me that he had to go to West Memphis so, him and Damian with and then I went with them.

RIDGE: Alright, when?

JESSIE: Wednesday

RIDGE: Alright, when did you go with them?

JESSIE: That morning

RIDGE: 9 o'clock in the morning?

JESSIE: Yes, I did. I went with them and then

GITCHELL: Now, where you in a car? Whose car where you all in?

JESSIE: We walked

GITCHELL: You all walked?

JESSIE: Right, we walked and then uh,

RIDGE: Where did you go?

JESSIE: We went up to Robin Hood

RIDGE: You went to the Robin Hood, explain to me where those woods are.

JESSIE: By uh, Blue Beacon Truck Wash.

RIDGE: A little patch of woods

JESSIE: A little patch of woods

RIDGE: Behind Blue Beacon?

JESSIE: Behind it, right there behind it.

RIDGE: okay, what occurred while you were there?

JESSIE: When I was there, I saw Damian hit these one boy real bad, and then uh, and he started screwing them and stuff and then uh,

RIDGE: Alright, you got in front of you a picture, that was taken out of the newspaper I believe, it's got three boys and these are the three boys that were killed on that date in Robin Hood Woods, okay, which one of those three boys is it you say Damian hit?

The third picture, which will be

JESSIE: Michael Moore

GITCHELL: This boy right here,

JESSIE: Yeah,

GITCHELL: Alright, that's uh the Byers boy, that's who you are pointing at?

JESSIE: Yes

RIDGE: If you read the caption, the grizzly slain from left, 8 year old Michael Moore, Steven Branch and Christopher Byers. Okay, so you saw Damian strike Chris Byers in the head.

JESSIE: Right

RIDGE: What did he hit him with?

JESSIE: He hit him with his fist and bruised him all up real bad, and then Jason turned around and hit Steve Branch

RIDGE: Okay

JESSIE: And started doing the same thing, then the other one took off, Michael Moore took off running, so I chased him and grabbed him and hold him, until they got there and then I left.

RIDGE: Alright, when you get the boys back together, where were you at from the creek?

JESSIE: I was up there by the Service Road

RIDGE: Up by the Service Road?

JESSIE: Yes

RIDGE: Okay, now when this, when he hit the first boy, where are they at when he hits him, are you in the woods, you're on the side of big bayou, you're out in the field, where were you at?

JESSIE: I was in the woods.

RIDGE: In the woods. Okay, you've been down there in those woods before, can you describe to me what in those woods, what's the location where you were?

JESSIE: Uh,

RIDGE: Is there a path that you go down?

JESSIE: Uh, down a little path

RIDGE: Alright, where does that path go too?

JESSIE: It leads out there close to the field,

close to the interstate.

RIDGE: Okay

JESSIE: Close to the interstate

RIDGE: When he hits the first boy and then Jason hits another boy, and one takes off running, where does he run too?

JESSIE: That one, he runs out, out the park and I chased him and grabbed him and brought him back.

RIDGE: Which way does he go, I mean, does he go back towards where the houses are, he's going to Blue Beacon, is he going out towards the fields, where's he running too?

JESSIE: Towards the houses.

RIDGE: Towards the houses?

GITCHELL: Where the pipe is that goes across the yards?

JESSIE: Yes, he run out there and I caught him and brought him back, and I took off.

RIDGE: Okay, and when you came back a little bit later, now are all three boys are tied?

JESSIE: Yes

RIDGE: Is that right?

JESSIE: Yes, and I took off and run home.

RIDGE: Alright, have they got their clothes on when you saw them tied?

JESSIE: No, they had them off.

RIDGE: They had already gotten them off. When he first hit the boy, when Damian first hit the first boy, did they have their clothes on then?

JESSIE: Yes

RIDGE: Alright, when did they take their clothes off?

JESSIE: Right after they beat up all three of them, beat them up real bad

RIDGE: Beat them up real bad, and then they took their clothes off?

JESSIE: Yes

RIDGE: And then they tied them

JESSIE: Then they tied them up, tied their hands up, they started screwing them and stuff, cutting them and stuff, and I saw it and turned around and looked, and then I took off running, I went home, then they called me and asked me, how come I didn't stay, I told them, I just couldn't.

RIDGE: Just couldn't stay

JESSIE: I couldn't stand it to see what they were doing to them.

RIDGE: okay, now when this is going on, when this is taking place, you saw somebody with a knife., who had a knife?

JESSIE: Jason

RIDGE: Jason had a knife, what did he cut with the knife. What did you see him cut or who did you see him cut?

JESSIE: I saw him cut one of the little boys

RIDGE: Alright, where did he cut him at?

JESSIE: He was cutting him in the face.

RIDGES: Cutting him in the face. Alright, another boy was cut I understand., where was he cut at?

JESSIE: At the bottom

RIDGE: On his bottom? Was he faced down and he was cutting on him, or

JESSIE: He was

GITCHELL: Now you're talking about bottom, do you mean right here?

JESSIE: Yes

GITCHELL: In his groin area?

JESSIE: Yes

GITCHELL: Okay

RIDGE: Do you know what his penis is?

JESSIE: Yeah, that's where he was cut at.

RIDGE: That's where he was cut.

GITCHELL: Which boy was that?

JESSIE: That one right there.

GITCHELL: You're talking about the Byers boy again?

JESSIE: Yes

GITCHELL: Okay

RIDGE: Are you sure that he was the one that was cut?

JESSIE: That's the one that I seen them cutting on.

RIDGE: Alright, you know what a penis is?

JESSIE: Yeah

RIDGE: Alright, is that where he was cutting?

JESSIE: That's where I seen them going down at, and he was on his back. I seen them going down right there real close to his penis and stuff and I saw some blood and that's when I took off.

GITCHELL: Was uh, where you all close to the creek at that point?

JESSIE: Yes sir

GITCHELL: Where was the little boy actually at?

JESSIE: He was close

RIDGE: Alright, now you know where the bayou is?

JESSIE: Right

RIDGE: Alright, and you know where the little Creek is that goes out to the express way, and it doesn't have a lot of water in it, but it's got some water in it, and it's flowing through the, which side of that creek were you on, where you on the Memphis side of the creek or the Blue Beacon side of the creek?

JESSIE: Blue Beacon.

RIDGE: On the Blue Beacon

JESSIE: Yes

RIDGE: So, there is like a tall bank, where were you at on that bank?

JESSIE: I was up there standing up there on the top.

RIDGE: Alright, where were they at?

JESSIE: They were at the bottom.

RIDGE: On which side?

JESSIE: Memphis side

RIDGE: They were on the Memphis side.

JESSIE: I was on

RIDGE: Alright, we're going to correct that even further, that's the east side, Memphis side is the east side and you were standing at the top of the bank on the west side, were you looking down at what was going on?

JESSIE: I was looking down, and after I seen all of that, I took off

RIDGE: Okay, and when you left, did you hear any more hollering or anything?

JESSIE: No

RIDGE: Alright, you went home and about

what time was it that all of this took place?

JESSIE: About

RIDGE: I'm not saying when they called you. I'm saying what time was it that you were actually there in the park?

JESSIE: About 12

RIDGE: About noon?

JESSIE: Yes

RIDGE: Okay, was it after school had let out?

JESSIE: I didn't go to school

RIDGE: These little boys

JESSIE: They skipped school

RIDGE: They skipped school?

JESSIE: They were going to catch their bus and stuff, and they were on their bikes and so,

RIDGE: Alright, they were on their bikes, where were the bikes at?

JESSIE: They laid their bikes down when they come out to the, when they hollered for them to come out there

RIDGE: Where did they lay their bikes

down at, that's what I'm asking you?

JESSIE: I don't know where they laid their bikes down at, cause I was behind Damian and nem, they were way behind them.

RIDGE: Okay

JESSIE: When they hollered, when they seen them boys

RIDGE: The little boys came on over?

JESSIE: Yes

RIDGE: Had Damian seen these boys before?

JESSIE: Yes

RIDGE: Has he done things with them before? Or had he just been watching them,

JESSIE: He had been watching them.

RIDGE: Has he ever had sex with them before?

JESSIE: No, he's been watching them

RIDGE: He's been watching them. You mentioned earlier that, one of the meetings you went to with this cult thing, they had some pictures. Describe those pictures for me.

JESSIE: They had some houses, trees and stuff
RIDGE: Okay, had somebody taken pictures of these boys?
JESSIE: Yes
RIDGE: Were they in the houses or were they in the trees when they took those pictures?
JESSIE: They were in the houses
RIDGE: At the houses? Did they take like one picture of one boy
JESSIE: They were in a group
RIDGE: All, these three
JESSIE: There was a group of pictures of all three of them.
RIDGE: All three of them would generally be together?
JESSIE: Yes
GITCHELL: How many pictures did you see, altogether?
JESSIE: I just saw one
GITCHELL: Okay, and it has these same three boys in it?

JESSIE: Yes

RIDGE: You're certain of that?

JESSIE: Yes

GITCHELL: Now, did you say that the boys skipped school that day, these little boys did?

JESSIE: Yes, they were going to catch, they were going somewhere and like I said, Damian and nem left before I did, I told them that I would meet them there and stuff, and it was early in the morning and so, they went ahead and met me, they went on up there and then I come up later on behind them.

GITCHELL: What time did you get there?

JESSIE: I got there about 9

GITCHELL: In the morning?

JESSIE: Yes

GITCHELL: Wednesday morning?

JESSIE: Yes

GITCHELL: And

RIDGE: What time is it right now?

JESSIE: Right now?

RIDGE: Yeah, you don't know what time it is?

GITCHELL: Do you not wear a watch?

JESSIE: It's at home

RIDGE: So

JESSIE: My dad woke me up this

RIDGE: so, your time period may not be exactly right in what you're saying?

JESSIE: Right

RIDGE: It was like earlier in the day, but you don't know exactly what time, okay, cause I've gotten some real confusion with the times that you're telling me, but now, this 9 o'clock in the evening call that you got, explain that to me.

JESSIE: Well after, all of this stuff happened that night, that they done it, I went home about noon, then they called me at 9 o'clock that night, they called me.

RIDGE: And what did they tell you on the telephone?

JESSIE: They asked me how come I left so early and stuff, and I told them that I couldn't stay there and watch that stuff no more, so I had to do something to get out of there.

RIDGE: okay, who called you?

JESSIE: Jason

RIDGE: And you mentioned that you heard some voice in the background?

JESSIE: I heard some dingling

RIDGE: And what else, I think you said that he made the call from his house?

JESSIE: He made the call from his house and Damian was hollering in the background saying, we done it, we done it, what are going to do if somebody saw us, what are we going to do?

RIDGE: Okay, the knives, was it one knife, two knives, was your knife there?

JESSIE: Ugh, ugh,

RIDGE: Now did somebody take it and used your knife, do you have a knife?

JESSIE: I got one knife

RIDGE: Where is it at?

JESSIE: It's at home

RIDGE: okay, the knife that you said Jason was using, where is it?

JESSIE: Uh, I don't know what he done with it, cause after I left then they, I don't know what they done with, after I left

RIDGE: He didn't tell you that he hid it somewhere?

GITCHELL: I've got a feeling here, you're not quite telling me everything, now you know that we're recording everything, so this is very, very important to tell us the entire truth. If you were there the whole time, then tell us that you were there the whole time, don't leave anything out. This is very, very important, now just tell us the truth.

JESSIE: I was there until they tied them up and then that's when I left, after they tied them up, I left.

GITCHELL: But, you saw them cutting on the boys,

JESSIE: I saw them cutting on them, and then

GITCHELL: So, what else left is there, after that?

JESSIE: They laid the knife down beside them and I saw them tying them up and then that's when I left,

RIDGE: Were the boys conscious or were they

JESSIE: They were unconscious then

RIDGE: Unconscious

JESSIE: And after I left they done more.

RIDGE: They done more

JESSIE: They started screwing them again

RIDGE: Okay, how were they screwing them when you saw them?

JESSIE: They, Jason stuck his in one them's mouth and Damian was screwing one of them up the ass and stuff.

RIDGE: Okay, and the one that they were cutting the penis off of, did any of them are cutting the penis or whatever was being done, did they have sex with them at all?

JESSIE: No

RIDGE: Did either one of them?

JESSIE: Jason did

RIDGE: Jason did?

JESSIE: Jason was screwing him while Damian stuck his in his mouth

RIDGE: Okay, how did he have sex with that one?

JESSIE: He was holding him down like, and Jason had his legs up in the air and that little boy was kicking, saying, 'don't, no' like that.

RIDGE: Okay, he had his legs up in the air, alright, what was to keep the little boys from running off, but just their hands are tied, what's to keep them from running off?

JESSIE: They beat them up so bad so they can't hardly move, they had their hands tied down and he sit on them

RIDGE: You said that they had their hands tied up, tied down, were they hands tied in a fashion that they couldn't have run, you tell me.

JESSIE: They could run, they just had them tied, when they knocked them down and stuff, they could move their arms and stuff, and hold them down like, wake up and raise up and the other one just put his legs up.

RIDGE: Okay, so they had them under control, you were there the whole time that was taking place?

JESSIE: I was there.

RIDGE: Okay, none [note: this is not clear - it may be 'one'] of them were cut on the face real bad, is that what you said?

JESSIE: Yes

RIDGE: And one of them was being cut on his penis?

JESSIE: Yes sir

RIDGE: Alright,

GITCHELL: Did you ever use, did anyone use a stick and hit the boys with?

JESSIE: Damian had kinda of a big old stick when he hit that first one, after he hit him with his fist and knocked him down and got him a big old stick and hit him.

GITCHELL: What did the stick look like, I mean was it like a big log like that or is it a stick?

JESSIE: I would say it was about that big around, I would say about that long.

GITCHELL: Okay

RIDGE: About the size of a baseball bat, maybe just a little bit bigger round?

JESSIE: Yeah

RIDGE: That's what you're describing with your hands, right?

JESSIE: Right

RIDGE: Okay, how long was the knife that Jason was using?

JESSIE: About that long

RIDGE: Alright, you're describing a knife that would be about 6 inches long, is that right?

JESSIE: Yes

RIDGE: And, what kind of blade did it have on it?

JESSIE: Uh, like a regular knife blade

RIDGE: Was it a knife that you fold up, or was it like a hunting knife?

JESSIE: It was

RIDGE: Just one piece

JESSIE: Just a fold up knife

RIDGE: It was a folding knife?

JESSIE: Yes

RIDGE: okay, uh does Damian have a knife?

JESSIE: No

RIDGE: He doesn't have one, he didn't have one that night?

JESSIE: He didn't have one that night

RIDGE: Did he borrow yours?

JESSIE: No, he didn't borrow mine.

GITCHELL: Did they have a briefcase with them?

JESSIE: No

GITCHELL: You didn't see a briefcase?

JESSIE: I didn't see a briefcase, not unless they left it there at that day before it happened, unless they left it there then but I didn't see one that day.

GITCHELL: Have you ever seen them with a briefcase before?

JESSIE: I've seen them once that night, I seen them with it that night.

GITCHELL: Okay, what is kept inside of that briefcase?

JESSIE: They had some cocaine, and a little gun

GITCHELL: Is that when you first saw the pictures of the boys?

JESSIE: yes, out there in Lakeshore

GITCHELL: And you saw the pictures in the briefcase?

JESSIE: Yes, I think when we had that cult.

GITCHELL: okay, now you have participated in this cult, right?

JESSIE: Yes

GITCHELL: How long have you been involved in it?

JESSIE: I've been in it for about three months.

GITCHELL: Okay, what is, tell me some of the things that you all do typically in the woods, as being in this cult.

JESSIE: We go out kill dogs and stuff and then carry girls out there.

GITCHELL: What do you all do with the

girls when you're out there?

JESSIE: We screw them and stuff

GITCHELL: Just everybody takes a turn

JESSIE: Everybody, and we have an orgee and stuff like that.

GITCHELL: okay

RIDGE: when you kill a dog, what do you do with that?

JESSIE: We usually skin it, then make a barn fire and eat it and stuff

RIDGE: okay, when you initiating somebody new come into a cult what actually is done to initiate that person into a cult?

JESSIE: We usually you know, kill an animals, you know, you have to know how to handle the meat and stuff, after we kill it to see if he knows, if he can't handle it, then he don't get in.

RIDGE: Okay, so he kills an animal, you mentioned earlier that he may have to eat part of that animal, what part of the animal would he eat?

JESSIE: Uh, the meat off of his leg.

RIDGE: The meat off of his leg.

JESSIE: If he can't eat it, then he don't get in.

RIDGE: Doesn't get into the cult?

JESSIE: No

RIDGE: Now these meetings, have they ever been violent, anybody gotten made and got into a fight?

JESSIE: No

RIDGE: Okay, the night you were in the woods, uh had you all been in the water?

JESSIE: Yeah, we've been in the water, we were in it that night, playing around in it.

RIDGE: You were playing around in the water, alright, what were you doing in the water?

JESSIE: Just

RIDGE: Besides just playing, the little boys, had they been in the water? Did they get into the water with you all?

JESSIE: No, they didn't get into the water with us

RIDGE: Okay, what were you doing in the water?

JESSIE: We were just sitting there, throwing stuff at each other,

RIDGE: were you all having sex?

JESSIE: No, I wasn't

RIDGE: You weren't?

JESSIE: No

RIDGE: Damian and Jason having sex?

JESSIE: They took turns going up under the water

RIDGE: Going up under the water, what were they doing up under the water?

JESSIE: They were sitting so far away, they were in the water, I would say about five to ten seconds, then come up and then the other one would go down

RIDGE: Okay, so they were just messing around in the water. They called for these boys to come over there?

JESSIE: Yeah, they seen them boys and then they hollered, Damien said, hey, the little boys come up there.

GITCHELL: Did they call them by name?

JESSIE: No, they just hollered at them, they slowed up.

GITCHELL: Where did the boys put their bikes?

JESSIE: Close to right where there before you come in and they laid them down right there, and after I left I don't know what they done with the bikes.

GITCHELL: You didn't do anything to the bikes at all?

JESSIE: No

GITCHELL: Are you sure

JESSIE: Positive

GITCHELL: You didn't touch the bikes?

JESSIE: I didn't touch them

RIDGE: You've been back to this place since that murder

JESSIE: Yes

RIDGE: Since it (unaudible) what did you do there? Be truthful.

JESSIE: I went down there and sit there, and after what they did to the boys, I just sit there

RIDGE: And did what?

JESSIE: Just thought, what happened to them real bad, just thought.

RIDGE: Okay

JESSIE: And I left and stuff, and walked home.

GITCHELL: When did you go back there?

JESSIE: Two or three days after it happened, and I left.

RIDGE: You were there by yourself?

JESSIE: I was there by myself.

RIDGE: Didn't you go there with some more boys once?

JESSIE: Me. David

RIDGE: That particular place?

JESSIE: No, not to that place

RIDGE: Are you willing to go down there with us and us having a camcorder and show us where these things took place? Would you do that?

JESSIE: Silent

RIDGE: Wouldn't have any problem with

that?

JESSIE: Not that I know of, I wouldn't

RIDGE: But you would be able to point out where these things took place?

JESSIE: Yes

RIDGE: Which way the boys came from and where you all were when he hollered for the boys and stuff like that, you wouldn't have a problem with that?

JESSIE: After the murder and stuff, I would say about two or three days later after it happened, I went down there and thought about it and I haven't been down there since.

RIDGE: Okay, let me ask you something, now this is real serious and I want you to be real truthful, and I want you to think about it before you answer it, don't just say yes or no, real quick. I want you to think about it. Did you actually hit any of these boys?

JESSIE: No

GITCHELL: Now, tell us the truth

JESSIE: No

RIDGE: Did you actually rape any of these

boys?

JESSIE: No

RIDGE: Did you actually kill any of these boys?

JESSIE: No

RIDGE: Did you see any of the boys actually killed?

JESSIE: Yes

RIDGE: okay, which one did you see killed?

JESSIE: That one right there.

GITCHELL: Now, you're pointing to the Byers boy again?

JESSIE: Yes

RIDGE: How was he actually killed?

JESSIE: He choked him real bad and all

RIDGE: Choking him? Okay, what was he choking him with?

JESSIE: His hands, like a stick, he had a bit old stick, kinda holding it over his neck.

RIDGE: okay, so he was choking him to the point where he actually went unconscious, so at that point, you felt like he was dead?

JESSIE: Yeah

RIDGE: Okay, did any of the other two boys, were you there when they were actually killed?

JESSIE: I don't know

RIDGE: You say that you got sick, so that's what you were saying, did you throw up or anything?

JESSIE: Yes

RIDGE: Where did you throw up at?

JESSIE: I got a little bit ways out of there and got half a mile up the road, is when I threw up, and couldn't hardly run and I just threw up.

RIDGE: When you left from there, did you leave running?

JESSIE: Yes

RIDGE: Were you hiding?

JESSIE: No, I didn't hide.

GITCHELL: Did you have some blood on your clothes?

JESSIE: I didn't have no blood, I didn't get close to them

GITCHELL: Were your clothes wet still?

JESSIE: Yes, they were damp

GITCHELL: Muddy

RIDGE: Alright, Insp. Gitchell touched on a point, real close, now what clothes were Jason wearing that day? That night?

JESSIE: He was wearing some blue jeans and boots, army boots like,

RIDGE: Army boots? And what kind of a shirt, you know everybody wears a special shirt with different things

JESSIE: He was wearing a mega death shirt

RIDGE: A mega death

JESSIE: Or maybe a metalica

RIDGE: Metalica shirt, alright, was he wearing a cap, anything like that?

JESSIE: No, he wasn't wearing anything like that

RIDGE: Alright, Damian, what was Damian wearing.

JESSIE: Damian had some black pants on, some boots and a black t-shirt.

RIDGE: Was anything on his shirt?

JESSIE: No

RIDGE: No kind of design or anything?

JESSIE: No, just black

RIDGE: These blue jeans that Jason was wearing, designer jeans, or were they old jeans, wore out, holes

JESSIE: They were wore out

RIDGE: What did they look like?

JESSIE: They had holes in them and the knees were cut

RIDGE: Holes in the knees. What color is Jason's hair? JESSIE: Blonde

RIDGE: Light blonde, or like a sandy reddish type blonde, do you know the difference?

JESSIE: It's like

RIDGE: Sandy colored blonde

JESSIE: Sandy colored blonde

RIDGE: okay, wearing blue jeans, he had on a metalica shirt, now this is a shirt that's got metalica across the front of it spelled out, and a man's name, or picture, is that right? You tell me.

JESSIE: They had picture

RIDGE: A picture of somebody

JESSIE: Different shirts, different types of shirts have different pictures

RIDGE: Well, which one did he have?

JESSIE: He had that uh, like a, skull like

RIDGE: A skull?

JESSIE: Yeah

RIDGE: Okay, what were you wearing that day?

JESSIE: I was just wearing regular blue jeans, my shoes

RIDGE: What kind of shoes were you wearing?

JESSIE: My uh, Adidas

RIDGE: Adidas tenns shoes?

JESSIE: Yes

RIDGE: What kind of shirt were you wearing?

JESSIE: I was just wearing a regular old greasy up t-shirt.

RIDGE: Okay, was it a designed shirt, like this bull type shirt, or was it just a plain

white, old
JESSIE: Plain white
RIDGE: Old t-shirt, where are these shoes at now?
JESSIE: A friend of mine, he borrowed them
RIDGE: Who is that?
JESSIE: Buddy Lucas
RIDGE: Buddy Lucas?
JESSIE: He borrowed them from me
RIDGE: The boots that Damian had on, are they army type boots too, or what kind of boots were they? I
JESSIE: Close like army type, not quite
RIDGE: Okay, they are black, is that right, they lace up?
JESSIE: Yes
RIDGE: Okay, and Jason's black and lace up?
JESSIE: Jason's were black up to, about knee
RIDGE: Oh, they come way up on him?
JESSIE: Yes

RIDGE: Okay, Damian's didn't come up that far?

JESSIE: No

RIDGE: Okay, they killed the boys, you decided to go, you went home, how long after you got home before you received the phone call? 30 minutes or an hour?

JESSIE: Uh, silent an hour

RIDGE: An hour after you got home, so they were there for a lot longer

JESSIE: Yes

RIDGE: When he called you on the phone, did he say that he had just got in?

JESSIE: When he first called me, he said, how come you left, and said, I couldn't stand it, I had to do something else

RIDGE: Okay, you couldn't stand it.

JESSIE: And then Damian, I heard Damian in the background saying we done it, we done it, what we gone do if somebody saw us

RIDGE: Did anybody see you leaving?

JESSIE: No

RIDGE: That you know of

JESSIE: That I know of

RIDGE: Did anybody see Damian and Jason?

JESSIE: I don't know, I left before them

RIDGE: But have you heard anybody say that they saw Damian and Jason?

JESSIE: No

RIDGE: You haven't heard anybody?

JESSIE: No

RIDGE: Okay, these initiations, you say that they eat part of the leg meat?

JESSIE: Yeah

RIDGE: Does that involve eating part of the penis of the animal?

JESSIE: No

RIDGE: Just the meat?

JESSIE: Just the meat

RIDGE: Okay, has Jason and Damian talked to you since this happened?

JESSIE: No

RIDGE: They haven't talked to you about this?

JESSIE: They hadn't said nothing around me, when I was over to my friend's house, they didn't say nothing.

RIDGE: When you've been by yourself, and I'm sure in the last three weeks you've been by yourself with them sometime

JESSIE: You know Damian keeps asking me how come I left and stuff and hadn't anybody said anything to me about it.

RIDGE: Okay, what did he say to you about it when you came to the police department, after seehng that boy in the woods? Up there behind the Goodyear place? What did he say about that?

JESSIE: He didn't know anything about that.

RIDGE: He doesn't know that

JESSIE: No

RIDGE: Okay, what about when you get with Jason by himself?

JESSIE: He keeps on asking me what are we going to do next, I told him, I can't do nothing now cause I go to work with my daddy everyday

RIDGE: So, they are scared, is that right,

JESSIE: They are scared cause after what they did, I told him that I was going to work with my daddy, I got to do something

RIDGE: So, what do you think ought to be done to them for killing these boys?

JESSIE: They need to be put away for awhile,

RIDGE: Put away for a while. Do you think they are sick or just mean?

JESSIE: I think they are sick

RIDGE: They are sick okay. Is there anything else that you want to add to this statement?

JESSIE: No

RIDGE: Why did you not come forward with this information?

JESSIE: Cause I was scared

RIDGE: Scared of Damian? or scared of the police?

JESSIE: Scared of the police

RIDGE: Are you scared of Damian now?

JESSIE: No

RIDGE: Are you scared of the police now?
JESSIE: No
RIDGE: You are not, so we've treated you well?
JESSIE: Yes
RIDGE: Alright, I am going to conclude this interview, the time is 3:18PM.

3:18 PM THE TAPED CONFESSION WAS COMPLETED. WORK WAS STARTED IN REFERENCE TO OBTAINING SEARCH WARRANTS AND ARREST WARRANTS FOR THE PERSONS NAMED AS PARTICIPANTS IN THE HOMICIDE.

3:22 PM JESSIE JR. OFFERED FOOD WHICH HE DECLINED AND WAS GIVEN TWO CIGARETTES.

[The word "Incorrect" is written in margin]
3:45PM INSPECTOR GITCHELL CONDUCTED A SECOND INTERVIEW

WITH JESSIE MISSKELLEY JR. TO CLEAR UP SOME DISCREPANCIES CONCERNING TIME AND EVENTS IN THE FIRST INTERVIEW.

5:05 PM JESSIE JR. ASKED IF HE WANTED ANY FOOD TO EAT.

6:15 PM JESSIE JR WAS FED.

6:30 PM JESSIE JR. WAS ASKED IF HE WANT TO RELIEVE HIMSELF.

9:06 PM RIDGE, GITCHELL, FOGLEMAN PRESENT FOR A PROBABLE CAUSE HEARING WITH JUDGE P. RAINEY PRESIDING.

9:14 PM TESTIMONY WAS GIVEN CONCERNING THE PROBABLE CAUSE FOR THE SEARCH WARRANTS AND ARREST WARRANTS FOR THOSE INVOLVED IN THE HOMICIDE.

Within two hours of the arrest warrants being issued, both Damien Echols and Jason Baldwin would be arrested and charged, along with Jessie Misskelley, with three counts of capital murder.

CHAPTER FIVE
JASON BALDWIN

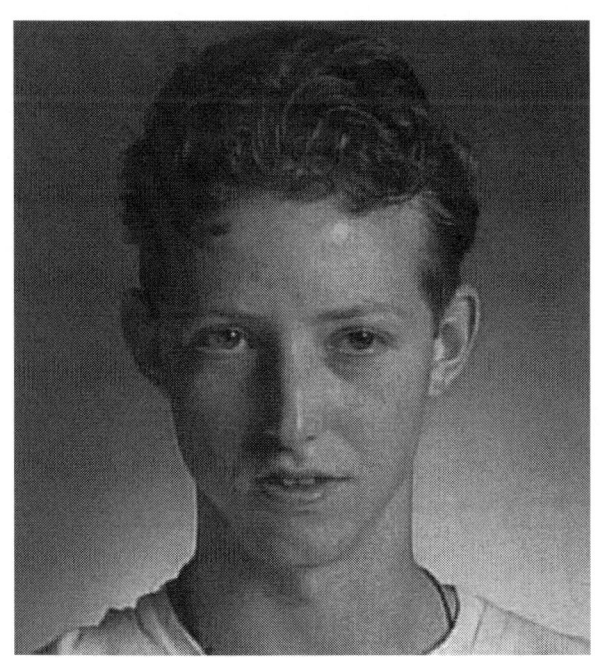

After the confession of Jessie Misskelley, one of those arrested and implicated in the murders was a sixteen year old local teen by the name of Charles Jason Baldwin. From the outside looking in, one might say that he was guilty only by association. But, as we dig further into the facts of this case, we begin to see that things may be different than they first appear.

Jason is the son of Larry Baldwin and Angela Baldwin Grinnell. His parents who are also second cousins, divorced when Jason was very young. Jason had a very challenging home life. Just three months before the murders;, Jason's mother was involuntarily hospitalized for paranoid delusions after Jason came home and found her bleeding from self-inflicted injuries and called 911.

Angela eventually met a new man named Terry Grinnell. They dated for a while then they decided to marry and try to be a family. But the relationship between Angela and Terry did not last long. Terry eventually moved out of the house and went to live at his mother's home. Jason was responsible for looking after his younger brother Matt and step-brother Terry Jr. now that his parents had separated.

Baldwin was on probation since he was 13 for criminal mischief and also had a more recent conviction for shoplifting in May 1993. When Damien Echols returned to Arkansas following a brief move to Oregon, Baldwin's grades and school attendance began to take a downward slide and he was warned that if he missed any more school it would violate his probation.

Angela met yet another man and after a short dating period she made the decision to allow him to move into her home with her and her boys. But just like her previous relationships, this one was also doomed to failure from the very start. On May 5, 1993, Angela and her live-in boyfriend, Dink Dent, had an altercation and she kicked him out of the house. It would be the very next day that the world would be informed of the brutal slayings of the three innocent little boys.

Within the next month, Angela would try to reconcile with her second husband Terry. Terry agreed to move back into the house and try to work things out with Angela.

On June 3, 1993, the night that Jason was arrested, Angela returned home from work to find that the WMPD was searching her home. She became hysterical and began screaming at Terry, accusing him of turning Jason in for the reward money. Jason was at Damien's house that evening. When the police went to Damien's to arrest the teenagers, the boys turned the lights out and went under the bed in a ridiculous attempt to hide from their fate.

Most people that I have spoken to say that they believe that Jason is 100% innocent. Unfortunately, the main stream media, TV documentaries and movies that were made about this case left out some very important and significant information regarding Jason Baldwin and the West Memphis murders.

Now before we go any further, again I will say that if you do not believe what I am writing here, I do ask that you search the case information online and review the information for yourself.

On Tuesday May 4th, 1993, the day before the murders, Jason Baldwin traded three of his heavy metal t-shirts for a curved "throwing" knife, and a mountain climbing ice pick to Billy Newell. On Friday, May 8, 1993, Jason had his little brother Matthew return those items. Jason had kept these items hidden under his bed for the last few days, claiming that *"somebody was going to accuse him of using them."*

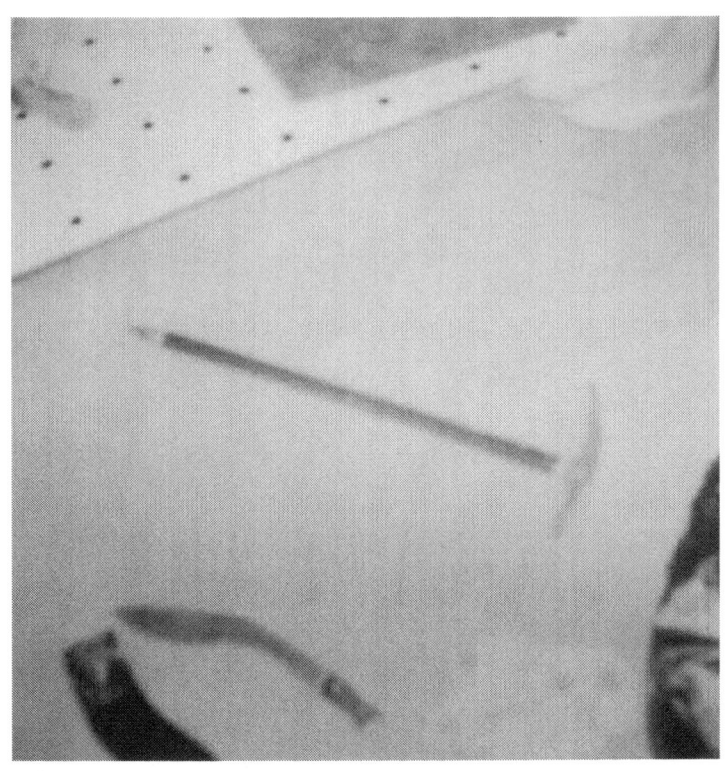

On May 11, 1993 Billy and Kenny Newell notified the West Memphis Police and turned the weapons over to them.

Kenny was interviewed by the West Memphis Police. Here is the statement that he gave them.

Statement of Kenny Newell (Billy Newell's brother)
Lakeshore Drive

Jason was over at our house and Billy wanted to
trade something for some shirts. And the only thing
Billy has good enough to trade is the weapons. Billy
picked the shirts he wanted and they traded. And 3
or 4 days later Jason's little brother brong the pick
and the nife back and got the shirts but we didn't
find the testement shirt so he still has it.

Jason Baldwin and his brother Mathew Baldwin
lives west from our house at the street right before
the last one by the fild 3 or 4 trailers down on the left.

Billy Newell is my brother. The first trade took place at the early part of last week. The second trade took place at the last part of the same week.

This statement was completed at 6:28PM on the 5-11-93

Billy Newell was also interviewed. During his statement he asked, "I wonder if these were the weapons that were used to kill the boys."

James William Thomas Newell III(Billy)
W/F 1-13-76
11 May 93 Lakeshore Drive
6:16 P.M. West Memphis, Ar

7**-**** (Mae Manuec)

I worked at the Carnival from Wednesday until Friday and I had three T-shirts that I had traded a pic and a knife for, to Jason Baldwin, before I worked at the Carnival. When I got home yesterday I found the pic and knife where Jason had brought it back. I mad the statement to some kids that "I wonder if these were the weapons that were used to kill the boys." Then I said maybe I'd better call up to the police and tell them. I know Damien and I think he's one of his own along with his sidekick, Jason. I don't belong to any gangs and just recently moved here from Forrest City.

6:25 P.M.

Sgt M.M. Kesterson
Bryn Ridge
003546

Because the pick axe and knife were not found in Jason's possession, the prosecutors were not able to bring them into the trial as evidence.

Because of this, the Newell brothers were never called as witnesses, and the pick axe was never mentioned in the media or any of the documentaries or movies. When we spoke to the original investigators on this case, they told us that had this information been made available to the public, they believed that people would not have been so quick to want to free Jason from prison.

Based on autopsy photos of the wounds on Michael Moore's head and the actions of

Jason Baldwin regarding the pick axe (*prior to him being indicated as a suspect*) one could possibly assume that these weapons could have been used in the commission of these murders.

Michael's body was taken to the Arkansas State Crime Laboratory Medical Examiner Division. Here is an excerpt of their report concerning the wounds to Michael Moore's head.

Frank J. Peretti, M.D. William Q. Sturner, M.D.
Assoc. Medical Examiner Chief Medical Examiner

Head Injuries:
Multiple punctate scratches were present over the bridge of the nose. The left ala was abraded. The left side of the cheek was contused and edematous, with an overlaying 1 1/2 inch contusion. The lips were abraded. The mucosal surfaces of the lips were contused, slightly edematous, with multiple superficial lacerations. The frenula were intact. Linear scratches were present on the left mandible region, along with a 3 by 3/4

inch area of abrasion.

Situated on the right frontal scalp was a 2 1/2 by 1/2 inch area of edema and ovoid contusion with overlying multiple small superficial lacerations and a 1/8 inch depressed abraded laceration. On the left forehead was a 1 5/8 inch by 1 1/8 inch abraded laceration. At the superior margin of this wound was a 1/2 inch abrasion. The anterior and posterior surfaces of the right ear were contused, with overlaying linear scratches. The helix of the right ear was abraded.

Situated on the right parietal scalp was an ovoid area of contusion with associated edema, measuring 2 3/4 inch by 1 1/2 inch.

On page 2 of this report the following head wounds are clearly noted:

Situated on the left parietal scalp was a dove-tail type laceration measuring 3/4 by 1/8 inch. At the inferior margin of the wound was an extension patterned contusion in the form of an upside down "L"; the vertical portion measured 1/2 inch and the horizontal portion measured 1/4 inch.

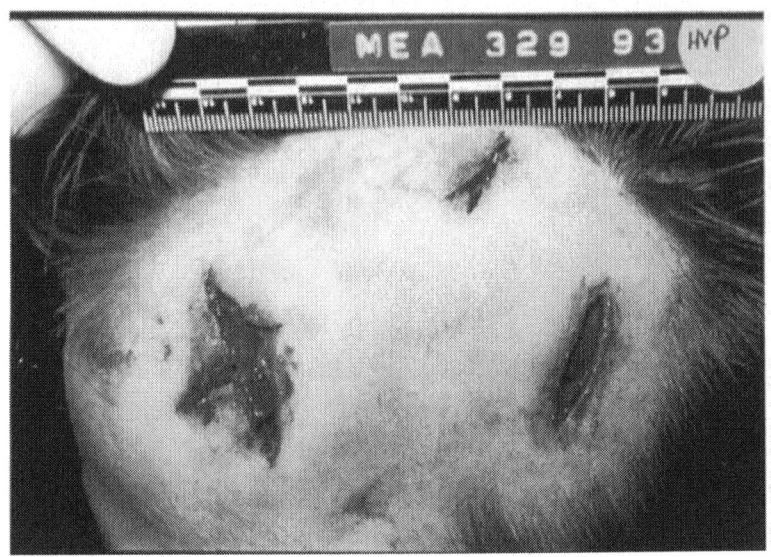

Wounds found on the head of Michael Moore

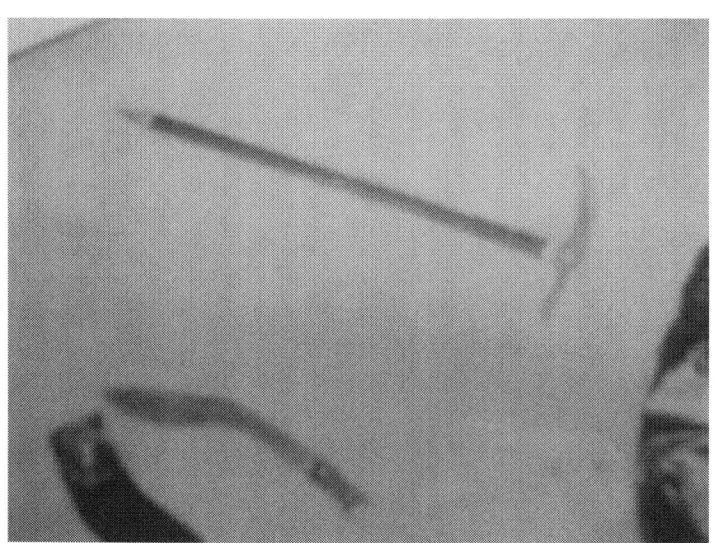

Actual Pick axe owned by Jason Baldwin

Similar axe image close up

Most people are not even aware that there was ever a pick axe involved. The main reason for that is because that evidence conflicted with what the main stream media wanted to be released and it goes against their personal biased opinions.

But regardless of the fact that Jason had in his possession a weapon that seems to correspond exactly to the wounds that were found on one of the victims, let's look at the alibi that Jason provided to police for the day that the three boys were killed. Unfortunately, Jason Baldwin never gave any statement as to his whereabouts on the evening of the killings. However, numerous other people gave statements to the West Memphis Police investigators concerning where Jason was on the day of May 5, 1993. But all of them would be shown to be false based on the facts that law enforcement had already gathered.

On June 4th, the day after Jason was arrested, Gail and Terry Grinnell, Jason Baldwin's mother and stepfather, told police that school records showed that Jason had taken the bus home from school around 3:00 or 3:30 PM on May 5. Then, Jason had gone to his uncle's home at 1037 Park Drive, in West Memphis, to mow his lawn from approximately 4:30 to 6:00 or 6:30 PM,. Jason had been accompanied by Ken Watkins and Damien Echols. After getting paid for mowing the lawn, Jason had taken his money that he had earned and gone with Ken to the local Walmart, and had gotten home sometime around 7:30 PM.

Here is an excerpt from the interview that Gail and Terry gave to Detective Ridge.

Det. Ridge: Okay. *What time did he get home that night?*

Angela Grinnell: *I think he got home about 7:30.*

Det. Ridge: 7:30. *Were you there?*

Angela Grinnell: *No sir, I have to, unfortunately I work at night. I wish I didn't have to but I have had to support my children.*

Neither Gail nor Terry Grinnell had actually seen Jason get home that night, because Gail had been at work and Terry was living temporarily with his mother.

On June 14th, the detectives spoke with Jason's uncle, Hubert Bartoush. He told the police that Jason had indeed mowed his lawn on Wednesday May 5th between 4:30 and 6:30 PM. However, he recalled that Jason had been alone, not accompanied by Damien or Ken.

STATEMENT OF: Hubert B. Bartoush
DATE: PAGE:
1037 Park W. Mphs.
DOB: 10-3-29 S/R [omitted]

On 5-5-93 Jason Baldwin, my Grand Nephew, came to my house at about 4:30 PM and mowed my yard. He was alone when he was at my house. He left my house at about 6:30 PM and said he was going to Walmart to play video games. I remember the times because Jeopardy was coming on when he got here and Wheel of Fortune was coming on when he left.

I have written this statement consisting of 1 page[s], and I affirm to the truth and accuracy of the facts contained therein.

This statement was completed at 1:56 PM., on the 14 day of June 1993.

WITNESS: Det. B. Ridge
Hubert B. Bartoush
WITNESS: Signature of person giving voluntary statement

This statement places Jason Baldwin within 1one mile of the crime scene on the day of the murders. I will add that this statement alone and the fact that his whereabouts after 6:30 PM could not be verified do not mean that Jason Baldwin murdered the boys. But what this statement does provide is proof that Damien's alibi for being at Jason's uncle's house on the day of the murders is at least flawed.

On September 23rd, Jason's mother, Gail Grinnell, again stated that Jason had mowed his uncle's lawn on Wednesday May 5, 1993, from 4:30 to 6:30 PM. She also stated that Jason was accompanied by Damien Echols, Domini Teer (Damien's girlfriend) and Ken Watkins. She also said that Damien and Domini had left first, then Jason and Ken had walked to Walmart to play video games, and then walked home. Also, on September 23rd, Jason's brother, Matthew Baldwin, told police that Jason came home that night at around 7:30 accompanied by Ken Watkins.

To some, this would seem like an air tight alibi. Jason's mother and brother both gave statements to the police that Jason was at home around 7:30 PM on the night that the crime happened. But Ken Watkins himself would give a totally different version of what happened on that afternoon in his September 16th interview. Watkins said that he, Damien, Domini and Jason had walked from Jason's house to Walmart around 4:00 PM that day, and that he (Watkins) walked back home alone around 5:30 PM to babysit. After his polygraph, Watkins added a detail to his earlier story stating that when he left Walmart at 5:30 that day, "They said they was going to the bowling alley." (Not clear who "they" included; he mentioned Damien, Jason, Domini and L.G. Hollingsworth being at Walmart before he left.)

Watkins also makes a statement in his interview about the actions of Jason and Damien following the murders. He stated that Damien told him that he had been present during the murders of the three eight year old boys.

These excerpts are taken from the interview that Watkins gave to Detective Ridge on September 16th.

KENNETH- YEAH. AND WE WERE SITTING THERE LISTENING TO SOME MUSIC AND PLAYING NINTENDO, SOME OF IT. THEN JASON'S MOM CALLS AND SAYS THAT THREE KIDS HAVE BEEN MURDERED, AND UH, BEHIND THE, UH, WOODS BACK THERE. BEHIND THE TRAILER PARK. THEN, NONE OF US BELIEVED IT. WELL, I DID, AND CARL DIDN'T. THEN, THE COPS CAME BACK, THAT CAME TO JASON'S HOUSE.

RIDGE- WHAT DID DAMION HAVE TO SAY ABOUT THAT?

KENNETH- DAMION DIDN'T SAY NOTHING. HE WAS JUST SITTING THERE BEING QUIET.

RIDGE- SO WHEN HIS MOTHER CALLED..WHEN JASON'S MOTHER

CALLED AND DAMION HEARD THE NEWS THAT THREE BOYS HAD BEEN KILLED, DID HE REACT AT ALL?

KENNETH- HE JUST SAT BACK THERE AND JUST DID NOTHING.

RIDGE- OKAY. WHAT OCCURS NEXT?

KENNETH- THEN, ABOUT TWO HOURS LATER, THE COPS CAME. HIS PROBATION OFFICER AND A COP CAME TO HIS HOUSE AND WANTED TO TALK TO HIM. THEN THEY ASKED WHERE HIS MOM WAS, AND SO I GUESS THEY WENT TO COURT THE NEXT DAY.

RIDGE- NOW YOU SAID HIM, AT THAT TIME YOU'RE TALKING ABOUT JASON?

KENNETH- YEAH, JASON. THE COPS TALKED TO JASON.

RIDGE-OKAY.

KENNETH- THEY WENT UP AND KNOCKED ON THE DOOR, AND ASKED IF JASON WAS THERE. AND JASON, IT WAS HIS PROBATION OFFICER. AND THEY WANTED TO TAKE HIM DOWNTOWN FOR QUESTIONING.

RIDGE- DOES STEVE JONES SOUND FAMILIAR, BEING THAT PROBATION OFFICER.

KENNETH- YES, I THINK IT WAS, I'M NOT POSITIVE.

RIDGE- NOW, YOU MENTIONED WHEN A TAPE WAS BROUGHT INTO THE HOUSE. WHEN DOES THAT OCCUR.

KENNETH- CARL BOUGHT, NEXT DOOR TO HIS HOUSE, THEY GOT A TAPE, AND HE CAME BACK AND ME AND HIM WENT IN THERE TO PUT IT IN. AND DAMION AND JASON WENT IN THE LIVING ROOM TO TALK.

RIDGE- OKAY, AND WHEN YOU CAME OUT OF THE BEDROOM...

KENNETH- THEY STOPPED TALKING AND STARTED TALKING ABOUT SOMETHING ELSE.

RIDGE- SO THEY WERE OBVIOUSLY TALKING ABOUT SOMETHING THEY DIDN'T WANT YOU TO HEAR.

KENNETH- YEAH.

RIDGE- IS THAT WHAT YOU'RE SAYING? OKAY. NOW, DID ANYTHING ELSE HAPPEN THAT DAY.

KENNETH- NUN UH.

RIDGE- OKAY. THE NEXT DAY ON FRIDAY.

KENNETH- FRIDAY, WE WAS WALKING...

RIDGE- OKAY, YOU SAY WE. WHO DO YOU MEAN, WE?

KENNETH- ME AND DAMION.

RIDGE- ALRIGHT, WHAT TIME WAS IT?

KENNETH- ABOUT 4. TO GET DOMINI.

RIDGE- OKAY. YOU WERE WALKING FROM...

KENNETH-...LAKESHORE CAUSE WE HAD TO GO GET...YEAH.

RIDGE- AND WHERE WERE YOU GOING?

KENNETH- WAL-MART.

RIDGE- OKAY.

KENNETH- THEN WE WALKED ON THE OVERPASS, WHICH DAMION, AND DAMION SAID THAT HE WAS THERE, AND A COUPLE OF OTHER FRIENDS. A FEW PEOPLE.

RIDGE- NOW WHAT'S HE TALKING ABOUT WHEN HE SAYS HE WAS THERE.

KENNETH- HE SAID THAT HE KNOWS WHO KILLED THE LITTLE KIDS, CAUSE HE WAS THERE, WITH A COUPLE OF PEOPLE.

RIDGE- OKAY.

In his first recorded statement on September 16th, Watkins said he had met up again with Damien, Domini and Jason around 7:00 PM on the evening of May 5th, at Jason's house. In his second recorded statement, Detective Ridge asked Watkins again if he had seen Damien and Jason that evening. Unfortunately, the answer that he gave would just bring more confusion than anything else.

Ridge- Okay. When you got home, and then you went back over to Jason's house, at what time?

Kenneth- About 6:45.

Ridge- And no one was there?

Kenneth- His mom's boyfriend. He said that they wasn't home yet. And I went back over there, finished watching the show. Then a little bit after that, I went over there to see if they were home ago.

Ridge- What was the show you were watching?

Kenneth- It was a movie.

Ridge- On T.V.?

Kenneth- Yeah.

Ridge- Was it a rental movie?

Kenneth- Huh uh. It was a movie on T.V. It's like a series.

Ridge- It's like a one hour show?

Kenneth- It's a half and hour show. Let's see, I watched Full House, then watched something else, and I went over there.

Ridge- What kind of movies do you normally like to watch on Wednesday evenings?

Kenneth- King-fu, and ...

Ridge- Timetracks?

Kenneth- No, I don't like Timetracks that much. I usually watch that, I don't even watch much T.V.

Ridge- 90210.

Kenneth- Uh uh.

Ridge- You don't like it?

Kenneth- I don't watch much T.V.

Ridge- Alright, did you watch Kung-fu...

Kenneth- Uh uh...

Ridge- That night?

Kenneth- I watched Bonanza. And then (inaudible) that Bonanza was on.

Ridge- Okay, how long were you there at Jason's?

Kenneth- Just about 2 hours.

Ridge- That evening.

Kenneth- Yeah. And when I got home, I went back over there and we stayed about 2 hours and I came home, and was watching Bonanza, and I watched part of it, and I went to sleep on the couch.

The relevant questions that Detective Ridge asked were: "Did you see Jason and Damien that evening? And if so, what time did they return to Jason's home?" The answers that Ken gave did not clarify those questions at all.

The statements that were given by Ken Watkins on September 16th were a major contradiction to the alibis that had been given for both Jason and Damien. Damien had stated that he was with his parents continuously from 3:45 PM onward that day, at home and at the Sanders' house. Jason's alibi was that he had mowed his uncle's lawn from 4:30 to 6:30 PM, then had gone to Walmart with Ken, and finally had walked home.

On June 11th, Jason's friend Garrett Schwarting told police that he had seen Jason at the Baldwin home around 7:00 pm on May 5. When police had spoken with him earlier on May 19, however, Schwarting had said that he had not seen Jason Baldwin in over three weeks. This was an ongoing challenge with the detectives' investigation. Numerous people would say one thing one day and in just a matter of a few days or weeks, their stories would completely change.

Even Jason Baldwin's own defense attorneys did not have very much confidence in Jason's alibi. During the trial proceedings, they did not call any alibi witnesses. The lead defense attorney, Paul Ford, defended his decision not to call any alibi witnesses at the Rule 37 hearings in 2008 by stating the following:

I concluded from my efforts that I did not find successfully what I was looking for, for the purposes of establishing an alibi that I felt would not unravel on me, which I believe is much more detrimental than not presenting one at all.

Some people do not even acknowledge the issue with Jason Baldwin's whereabouts on the day of the murders. Jason's lack of an alibi made the case against him that much stronger. During the process of researching this book, our team has been confronted by numerous people who claim that they know exactly where Jason and Damien were on the day of the murders. But when we asked for them to provide us with that information so that we could verify the facts, they simply refused to.

Paul Ford's decision not to present an alibi for Jason at trial was probably a smart move on his part. He knew that whatever alibi that the defense team presented would have been torn apart by the prosecutor. He decided to attack the prosecutor's case and try to present reasonable doubt to discredit the prosecution rather than tell the jurors where Jason was on the day of the murders.

Paul Ford said, *"And if I can [poke holes in the prosecution case and establish reasonable doubt], without exposing my client to cross-examination or if I can do that without placing witnesses on the stand to provide an alibi that I believe is a house of cards that may come tumbling down on me, I prefer that method".*

Even the defense admitted that Jason did not have a single credible alibi for his whereabouts on the evening of May 5, 1993. Paul Ford even made a statement to that fact. *"I'd like to believe I'm an ethical, honest lawyer and I cannot imagine, as much as I wanted to see Jason go free, because as much as I believed in his innocence, that I would ever unilaterally, cavalierly make a decision to not put on an alibi witness when he asked me to, if I thought I had one that would stand up".*

We all want to believe that a defendant is innocent until proven guilty and that every defendant deserves a fair trial and to have their day in court. In our country, it is the great responsibility of the State or the prosecuting attorneys to present their case to a jury in a court of law and to prove beyond a reasonable doubt that the person accused is indeed guilty of the crime with which they have been charged.

During the trial the prosecutor presented the State's case against Jason Baldwin. Jason's defense team tried very hard but they were not able to place Jason anywhere besides where the prosecutor claimed he was. To the shock and dismay of many, it seemed that Jason had indeed been in the Robin Hood Hills area on the night of May 5, 1993, helping in the brutal murders of Michael Moore, Steve Branch and Christopher Byers.

CHAPTER SIX
JESSIE MISSKELLEY
CONFESSIONS AND TRIAL

The trials for Jessie Misskelley, Damien Echols and Jason Baldwin took place in early 1994. Jessie Misskelley was tried separately, and Echols and Baldwin were tried together.

Jessie's trial began in the third week of January and ended on February 4th. Because Jessie decided not to testify in court against Damien and Jason, his confession could not be admitted against his co-defendants. The problem was that even though Jessie admitted to committing the crimes with Damien and Jason, his confession could not be entered into the trial due to the fact that the defense attorneys for Damien and Jason would not have a chance to cross examine Jessie. This is called the "Bruton Rule". Because of this issue, it was determined by the judge that Jessie would be tried separately.

During Misskelley's trial, Dan Stidham (Jessie's Lead Defense Attorney) was able to secure the expert testimonies of Dr. Richard Ofshe, an expert on false confessions and police coercion and Professor of Sociology at UC Berkeley. Ofshe testified that the brief recording of Misskelley's interrogation was a "classic example" of police coercion. After reading the confession and listening to the tape and interviewing Jessie Misskelley, Dr. Ofshe truly believed that Jessie's confession was a coerced and false confession. Dr. Ofshe gave the following reasons for this conclusion:

Nearly three hours of the interview was not recorded. Due to that fact, many people believe that the police used this time to create a scenario for Jessie to use as a confession to match the facts of the crime.

There were many instances of coaching from the interrogating officers, especially in regard to the timing of events. Jessie first stated that the crimes happened around noon. But with the coaching of the interrogators he was able to change his own time frame.

Many areas of Jessie's confession were not supported by the facts of the case.

Here are some of the key things that Jessie "confessed" to that were proven to be completely false.

Please note that some of this information was already discussed in chapter 4. But we feel like it is important to go over this again as a reminder so that it will be easier to follow along with what is being testified to at the trial.

Jessie stated that all three victims as well as Jason Baldwin were not in school on the day of the murders. It was proven by the investigators that they all were indeed in school all day on May 5, 1993.

Jessie stated that the victims were bound with rope when in fact they were bound with their own shoelaces. It is hard to believe that someone could have mistaken "rope" for shoelaces. If Jessie was in fact at the crime scene, then surely he would have known that the shoelaces were removed from the shoes and used to tie the boys.

Jessie stated that one boy was choked with a stick. After the autopsies the medical examiner's report stated that there was no evidence of strangulation.

Even if you overlook the previous inconsistencies in Jessie's statements up to this point, the next statement should have thrown up tons of red flags to the investigators.

Jessie stated that the boys were anally raped. It was determined by the medical examiner that NO EVIDENCE of sexual intercourse was discovered with ANY of the three victims.

Unfortunately, Dr. Ofshe was not permitted to state all of his opinion during the trial. Judge Burnett had previously ruled that Jessie's confession had been voluntary and Dr. Ofshe's testimony in this regard would directly contradict the court's previous ruling.

Burnett also stated that such a testimony would give an expert witness the power to determine whether the accused was guilty or innocent which was solely the responsibility of the jury. When it was all said and done, the jury only heard that Ofshe had a lot of experience with coerced confessions and it was possible for police to obtain a confession from someone who was in fact innocent. Anything more specific about Jessie's confession was not allowed.

The second expert witness to testify on Jessie's behalf was Warren Holmes, an expert with over 30 years of experience in ploygraph testing and interrogation techniques.

Judge Burnett ruled that Warren Holmes could not testify regarding the polygraph examination itself. This decision was made because polygraph test results are not admissible evidence in a court of law. He would only allow Holmes to testify to his experience and qualifications and to give his analyses of the interview techniques used during Jessie Misskelley's interrogation.

Holmes analyzed the polygraph test conducted by the WMPD on Jessie Misskelley and he found that Jessie's responses to the questions relating to the murders indicated that Jessie was truthful in his answers and in fact did not have any knowledge of them. The WMPD interrogating officers' statement to Jessie that he was in fact lying made Holmes believe that they had either not conducted or interpreted the results of the tests properly. Being informed that he was lying would have greatly contributed to Jessie's sense of helplessness in the situation and more than likely would have caused him to comply with the demand for a confession by the police. But Jessie did not know the facts of the crime well enough to give the West Memphis police detectives a confession that was credible.

According to Holmes there are a number of things that investigators look for to determine if a suspect's confession is in fact true.

In a true confession, the suspect will often give the police information about the crime that the police do not already know. In the case of Jessie Misskelley, all of the relevant information regarding the case that he knew was already public knowledge through newspapers and other media. The in depth facts surrounding the case that only the killer would have known was not accurate at all. Also the statements that Jessie made regarding the rope and the rapes did not fit the evidence of the crime. If a suspect is giving a true confession, there is no need for the police to correct the suspect on any contradicting details of the crime; and there is never a need to coach or lead a suspect for information. If the suspect is giving a true confession, the facts given by the suspect will fit the crime 100%.

A suspect would also give details in narrative form that include many minor details that the police have not discovered yet during the investigation process. Jessie was not able to add any more information to his confession than what the WMPD had already knew. Another aspect of a true confession is if the investigators make an incorrect statement regarding the crime, the suspect will correct them and give them the correct facts. They always want to take credit for every specific thing that they do when committing their crimes.

Holmes said that he was especially concerned that Jessie was wrong about the time frame and the type of ligatures used. Holmes also believed that both of these facts are things that the true killer could not make a mistake about. Jessie also failed to mention anything about how he was feeling at the time the crime was taking place or any time immediately afterwards. He also did not mention anything about the things that were being said by either himself, the other perpetrators or the victims as the crime was being committed.

Many experts agree that Jessie's confession was created by a series of highly suggestive questions by the interrogating officers and were not given in a narrative form by a person who was actually at the crime scene during the murders.

Unfortunately, the strongest evidence that the defense had to refute the prosecution's case was the very limited testimonies of these two expert witnesses.

The prosecutors felt confident that they had a strong case, which was built solely upon Jessie's confession. Some experts say that without the defense's expert witnesses, Jessie's case did not stand a chance.

Many people have asked if Jessie actually had an alibi for the day that the boys were murdered. What we do know is that the boys were seen with Terry Hobbs around 6-6:30 pm by a neighbor.

Witnesses also place Jessie at the Highland Trailer Park over 2 miles away from the crime scene for most of the day.

2:00 PM - Ricky Deese's wife sees Jessie in Highland Trailer park.

3:30 PM - 7:00 PM - Jessie with Susie Brewer at Highland Trailer park.

5:00 PM - 6:30 PM - Jessie and Susie went over to visit Stephanie Dollar at Dollar's trailer. (Which is also in the Highland

Trailer park)

6:30 PM - Jessie and Susie go outside to see police officers.

Stephanie Dollar had a situation where the local police had to be involved. Jessie was present when the police officer arrived at 6:30 PM.

Stephanie Dollar was interviewed by Detective Burch regarding the whereabouts of Jessie on May 5th. Following is a portion of that interview.

BURCH - ON THE 5TH? OKAY, WHERE DID YOU SEE HIM AT 6:30 ON THE 5TH?

DOLLAR - DOWN HERE AT THE CORNER WHERE THE FIRST STREET YOU CAN COME INTO

BURCH - THE AUTOMOTIVE SHOP?

DOLLAR - OKAY, DOWN AT THE STOP SIGN OVER HERE

BURCH - OKAY

DOLLAR - I SEEN HIM RIGHT THERE UP IN THAT AREA

BURCH - WHAT WAS HE DOING?

DOLLAR - HE STANDING BY A POLICE CAR

BURCH - A POLICE CAR AT 6:30 ON THE 5TH

DOLLAR - ON THE 5TH

BURCH - WAS IT A COUNTY CAR OR STATE CAR DO YOU KNOW?

DOLLAR - I HAD A REPORT, I HAD TO GO GET MY REPORT, SO I COULD REMEMBER I WORKED THAT DAY, BECAUSE I WASN'T FOR SURE IT WAS THAT DAY, I KNEW I HAD SEEN HIM THAT DAY BUT I WASN'T FOR SURE. SO I WENT UP MARION'S SHERIFF'S OFFICE AND UH, I GOT MY REPORT

AND ON IT, IT SAYS 05-05-93 IT SAYS WHAT TIME THE CALL WAS MADE AND WHAT TIME THE POLICE OFFICER ARRIVED AND IT WAS 6:30. BUT I HAD TO CALL THEM LIKE THREE TIMES BECAUSE THE FIRST TIME THEY CAME STRAIGHT TO MY HOUSE AND THEN THEY LEFT AND I CALLED BACK TO TELL THEM I WAS DOWN THE STREET AND HE TOLD ME TO MEET HIM AT THE CORNER AND THEN SEC, THIRD TIME I CALLED THEM WAS THE MAN. A INCIDENT HAD HAPPENED WHERE A LADY HAD SLAPPED MY LITTLE BOY IS THE REASON I HAD TO CALL THE POLICE IN THE FIRST PLACE.

BURCH - OKAY.

DOLLAR - WELL THE MAN GOT MAD THE WOMAN'S HUSBAND GOT MAD BECAUSE WE WERE GOING TO HAVE HER, HIS WIFE ARRESTED, AND HE GOT MAD AND CAME OVER THERE AND CUSSING AT MY HUSBAND AND TELLING HUSBAND HE WAS GOING

TO WHIP HIS BUTT AND ALL OTHER STUFF. HIM AND MY HUSBAND GOT INTO IT. I THOUGHT YOU KNOW OH, NO YOU KNOW BECAUSE THE GUY HAD A SHOVEL AND MY HUSBAND WAS GOING (INAUDIBLE) YOU KNOW YOU GET MAD. AND SO I WENT AND CALLED THE POLICE AGAIN WHEN THE POLICE COME IT WAS LIKE A 5 MINUTE SPAN BETWEEN THE 6:30 CALL TELLING THE POLICE OFFICER WHY AND LEFT OKAY. SO I SENT JIM. THERE WAS LIKE THREE COP CARS THAT CAME, AND I BELIEVE I DON'T KNOW THE OTHERS BECAUSE THEY AIN'T CAME AND TALKED TO ME, BUT I BELIEVE ONE OF THE OFFICERS NAME WAS STONE. ALRIGHT I TOOK JESSIE UP THERE TO THE CAR SO HE COULD HEAR WHAT THE LADY WAS SAYING ABOUT ME AND HE COME BACK AND TOLD ME WHAT SHE SAID. THATS HOW I KNEW HE WAS THERE AROUND THAT TIME.

BURCH - OKAY, AND THIS WAS ON WHAT DATE?

DOLLAR - THE 5TH OF MAY. ALRIGHT EARLIER THAT DAY I HAD A PARENT, TEACHER CONFERENCE WITH A DOCTOR MEGRUE AND MY LITTLE BOYS READING RESOURCE TEACHER WHICH IS UH, MRS. PURIFOY AND JUSTIN'S REGULAR TEACHER WHICH IS A MRS. STUART. AT 3 O'CLOCK THAT DAY AND I HAD TO HAVE JESSIE WATCH THE KIDS, I LEFT HERE ABOUT 2:30. AND I GUESSIN' I GOT BACK BETWEEN 3:30 AND 4. BECAUSE I HAD TO HAVE SOMEONE HERE TO MAKE SURE MY OTHER KIDS GOT OFF THE BUS. AND I HAD JESSIE WATCH THEM BETWEEN THAT TIME.

BURCH - AND THIS IS ON THE 5TH

DOLLAR - THE 5TH OF MAY

Detective Burch then asks Stephanie as to why Jessie would say that he had killed the boys.

BURCH - OKAY, WHY DO YOU SUPPOSE THAT JESSIE SAID THE THINGS HE DID THEN?

DOLLAR - I DO NOT KNOW, I REALLY DO NOT KNOW. I HONESTY DON'T KNOW. THAT IS WHAT IS SO CONFUSING TO ME, YOU KNOW. I KNOW HE WAS HERE AT 6:30, SUPPOSEDLY I DON'T KNOW THE TIME OF DEATH OF THE LITTLE BOYS. YOU KNOW, I DON;T KNOW ANY OF THAT ALL I KNOW IS WHAT I HAVE READ IN THE PAPER. YOU KNOW SO WHEN I SEE THAT THESE LITTLE BOYS UH, COME UP MISSING BETWEEN 5 AND 6, YOU KNOW IT KINDA, YOU KNOW YOU THINK WELL IT HAD TO HAPPEN AROUND THAT TIME YOU KNOW WHAT I'M SAYING. UH, AND THEN I KNOW HE WAS HERE AT 6:30 IT'S VERY VERY CONFUSING.

But what Stephanie did not know was that the boys were in fact killed later than 6:30PM on the 5th. We know this because a neighbor stated that the boys were seen in her yard and with Terry Hobbs at 6:30 pm on that day.

6:30 PM - Jessie is seen by: Louis Hoggard at the Highland Trailer park (who talks with him), Charles Ashley, Susie Brewer, Jennifer Roberts, Stephanie Dollar, Christy Jones, and Dennis Carter.

6:45 PM - Jessie and Susie got to Johnny Hamilton's house and the three walk back to Jessie's house.

7:00 PM - Jessie, Susie, and Johnny run into Jennifer and Christy at Jessie's house.

7:15 PM - Jessie walks Susie to Stephanie's house and walks back to his house to get mask. Jessie Sr. arrives home from DWI school.

7:15 PM - 7:30 PM - Jessie leaves for Dyess Arkansas with Freddy Revelle, Bill Cox, Roger Jones, Dennis Carter Jr., and Johnny Hamilton.

8:00 PM - Jessie and company meet Keith Johnson at Exxon station near Turell to go to Dyess. This service station is over 15 miles away from the crime scene.

8:00 PM - 12:00 AM - Jessie wrestling at Dyess AR. (about 35 miles from the crime scene) with: Bill Cox, Dennis Carter, Roger Jones, Johnny Hamilton, and Keith Johnson.

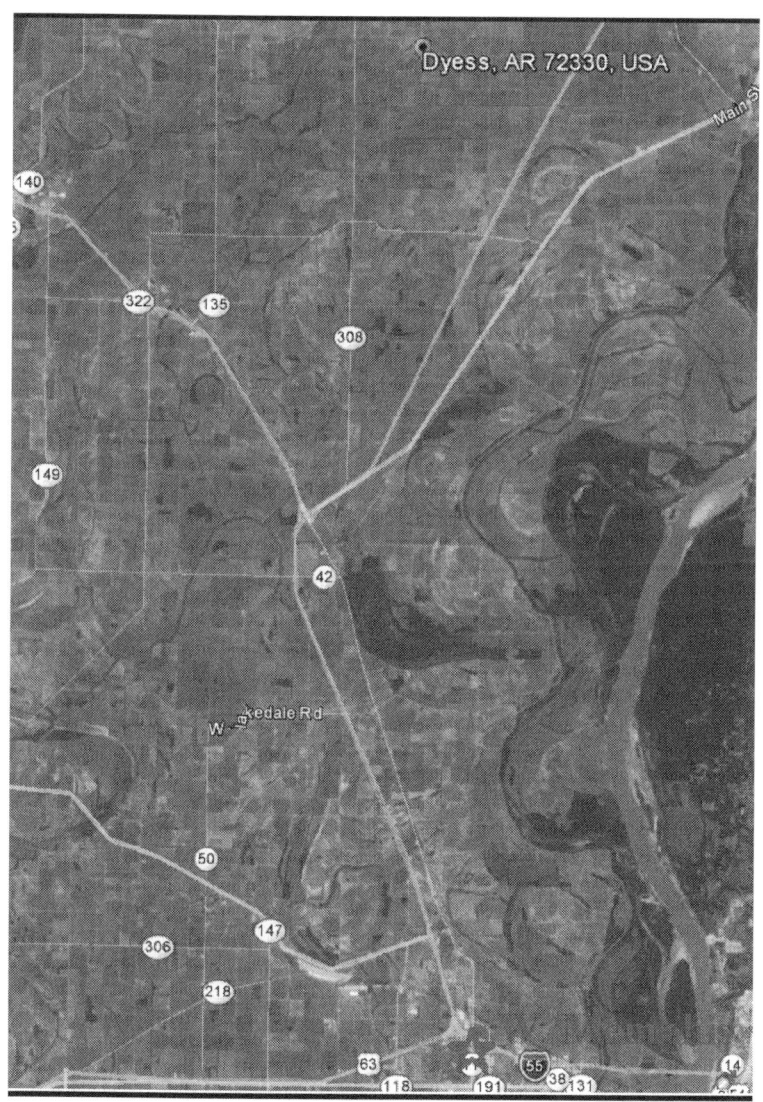

Freddy Revelle gave a statement to Detective Durham on June 9th regarding his whereabouts on May 5th.

DURHAM - WOULD YOU ACCOUNT FOR ME NOW AT THIS TIME THE INFORMATION YOU HAVE CONCERNING JESSIE MISKELLEY PLEASE?

REVELLE - YES SIR. I LIKE AROUND 7 O'CLOCK OR 7:30 WE WERE GETTING READY TO GO DYESS, ARKANSAS TO AN AH WE WERE PURCHASING A RING FROM THIS GUY THAT OWNS AN OLD THEATER BUILDING IN DYESS, ARKANSAS.

DURHAM - NOW WHAT DATE WAS THAT?

REVELLE - AH, IT WAS MAY 5TH. THE DAY OF THE MURDERS, AROUND 7 O'CLOCK, 6:30, 7 O'CLOCK, BILL COX THE GUY I'M TRAINING TO WRESTLE. HE ARRIVED AT MY RESIDENCE WITH THE MONEY THAT WE NEEDED

TO GO PAY THE CHARLES STONE IN DYESS FOR THE RING. I'M TRAINING HIM TO BE A PRO WRESTLER, TEACHING HIM WE LEFT AND PICKED UP JESSIE IN HIGHLAND TRAILER PARK. AND WE WERE GOING TO GET HIGH ON THE WAY UP THERE. AND AH WE PICKED HIM UP AND AH I'D SAY IT WAS AROUND 7 O'CLOCK I GUESS ABOUT THE TIME WE LEFT TO GO UP THERE. I DON'T KNOW EXACTLY WHAT TIME WE GOT THERE BUT WE GOT THERE AND AH ITS ABOUT 35 MILES, AND WE GAVE CHARLES STONE THE MONEY AND HE WROTE US OUT A RECEIPT AND GAVE US THE KEYS TO THE BUILDING SO WE COULD GET IN WENT BACK INSIDE HIS HOUSE WE OPENED UP HIS BUILDING AND WENT ON IN AND WE HAD TO TURN THE LIGHTS ON AND WE STARTED PRACTICING. WE LEFT AND I BELIEVE WE DROPPED LITTLE JESSIE OFF ABOUT 11:00, 11:30. THEN AH

DURHAM - NOW, WHEN YOU SAY

LITTLE JESSIE ARE YOU TALKING ABOUT JESSIE AH, MISSKELLEY?

REVELLE - JESSIE MISSKELLEY, JR. I'VE ALWAYS KNOWN HIM AS LITTLE JESSIE.

What is hard to understand is why Jessie would give a statement to the detectives that he was at the scene of the crime when so many people could place him someplace else.

And these people also testified at Jessie's trial about his whereabouts on May 5th. Some people believe that the overwhelming media attention and the ties to the satanic cult made this case a "slam dunk win" for the State.

One person that we spoke to regarding this case said that she believed that we need to take into consideration that Jessie wanted to be a professional wrestler. In this role he could be something that he never was: and that is "famous". Maybe Jessie admitted to killing these three boys because he wanted to be famous. For the world to know who he was, even if he did not do it.

When we look at the case we see on one side three little boys that were only eight years old murdered and mutilated. And on the other side, we see a teenager who confessed to helping kill these boys. Some people believe that Jessie Misskelley never stood at having a fair trial, and that his own words, even if they were coerced, were his worst enemy.

Jessie also made a statement to Deputy James Lindsey and Deputy Jon Moody while being transported back to the jail after his conviction. Jessie was in the transport vehicle heading back to the Arkansas Department of Corrections at Pine Bluff when he was asked if there was anything he wanted to say. Both deputies assured Jessie that they would not use anything he said against him in court. Jessie decided to tell the deputies what happened on the day of the murders. Deputy Jon Moody did in fact make a report for Inspector Gitchell at the WMPD regarding this conversation.

Time: 9:00 AM Report No. 1-6
Reporting Officer: Jon Moody
Area of Incident: Transport to ADC
Prisoner: Jessie Miskelley
Prisoner Number: N/A

Narrative:

To: Inspector Gitchell
West Memphis Police Department

From: Clay County Sheriffs Department

The following statement is a narrative as
told to Deputy James Lindsey and myself.
This statement is not in chronological order
as it was given by Jessie but has been put in
order to the best of our ability with
knowledge of your case. Your department
may have knowledge of this in its entirety, if
not, mabey it will provide a little insight as
to what took place on May 5th 1993.

Jail Incident Report

On the afternoon of Feb. 4th 1994, Deputy James Lindsey and myself were transporting Jessie Miskelley to the Arkansas Department of Corrections at Pine Bluff. Jessie was asked if there was anything he wanted to say and after being assured we could not use anything he said against him in court, he chose to talk.

Jessie advised he had received a call from Jason Baldwin asking him if he wanted to go to West Memphis to "get some girls." Jessie, Damion, and Jason met on a local road on May 5th (sometime that evening). Jessie claimed that he had been drinking Evelyn Williams whiskey that Mrs. Hutchson had bought him and Jason and Damion were drinking beer. It was also stated that they had smoked two marijuana joints that afternoon. Jessie said that he had known Jason Baldwin since the 6th Grade and did not know Damion that well but that Damion would drink human blood remembering a time when Jason was bleeding and Damion took some of the blood with his finger and licked it off. Jessie stated that Officer Callahan had lied in Court about not seeing him on May 5th, Jessie claims they had a short conversation. After all meeting on the road, the three boys walked to the woods and were sitting in the water with Jason and Damion "going under," Jessie said he could not go under because of his ear problem.

The three young boys were seen from a distance when Damion told Jessie and Jason to hide. Jessie said they were hiding behind bushes when Damion grabbed Michael Moore. The two other young boys started hitting Damion trying to help their friend and that is when Jessie and Jason jumped out and helped Damion "beat them." Jessie advised he helped hold them and beat them but had no part in raping or killing them.

Jessie advised two of the boys were raped from behind before and after they were tied up and that Damion and Jason were taking turns with the two boys. Jessie said the boys were still alive at this time.

Jessie said the boys were kept quiet by putting hands over their mouths and that Jason and Damion had used "shirts" and that times their face was pushed down into the ground.

Jessie was asked how the boys were kept under control while being raped and not tied yet and he stated "They were like puppies, when you whoop a puppy and tell it to stay, it will." Jessie did say he had to catch Michael Moore but did not say at what point.

Jessie claims that the third boy was never raped but that he may have been the one that Damion took his penis and put it in his mouth (the young boys penis). Jessie said at one point Damion and Jason had one of the boys in a headlock with one he believed had his penis in the boys mouth while the other one had him from behind. Jessie said he did not mention the "ears" to the police, only a headlock. Jessie also mentioned that "sticks" had been used to beat the boys.

At one point, Jessie said that Jason had a "bucktype locking knife" and "cut it all off and threw it in the weeds" saying the boy was alive and tied at this point and that he was surprised blood did not get on him because blood went everywhere and he was about a "car length" away. Jessie said "they" threw him into the water and "he was still squriming around in the water" at which point he left. Jessie said he does not know what happened to the knife. Jessie said he believed the other two boys were not conscious when he left but were not in the water.

Jessie also stated that Jason called him "later" and asked him why he left and he told them he could not watch it any longer. He claims the only other contact with Jason and Damion were a couple of times at the skating rink but they were mad at him.

To this day, no one is sure why Jessie made this statement to the deputies on that day. Some say that it was a true confession as to what happened on the day of the murders.

But, Jessie not only confessed to the police about the murders; he also told inmates that he was incarcerated with that he had committed the murders. He even went as far as telling his own lawyer (Dan Stidham) that he committed the murders, while he swore on a Bible.

The weekend after his confession and arrest, Jessie Misskelley sent his family a letter from jail. In his letter to them he denies the charges. Here is a portion of what he wrote: "Ya'll know I did not do it. I am not that crazy. ... I hope that ya'll don't hate me because I did not do it. I was with Rickey Deese the day it happen."

On June 11ᵗʰ he met with his defense lawyer Dan Stidham. But for some reason when he met with his lawyer he told him the same story that he told the police. Dan Stidham discussed his first meeting with Misskelley for a 1996 *Arkansas Times* article entitled "John Grisham, meet Dan Stidham" (which Stidham reprints on his personal website).

Here is a portion of that article: [Jessie Misskelley] told the lawyers three important things that day. One, yes, he was there when the murders occurred. Two, the police had told him he was going to die in the electric chair (never mind that Arkansas no longer used that form of capital punishment). And three, when Stidham asked him to tell which of the three victims was castrated; Misskelley insisted that it was the blond boy, which was wrong.

Dan Stidham took detailed notes during a June 11, 1993, meeting with Jessie Misskelley. During Stidham's testimony at the Baldwin/Misskelley Rule 37 hearings, Kent Holt (Arkansas Assistant Attorney General) asked Stidham to read those notes. Here's that testimony, with quotations from Stidham's 6/11/93 notes bolded.

HOLT: Okay. I show you what's been marked as State's Exhibit 12E and ask if you can identify that document?

STIDHAM: (Witness examining same.) Yes, sir.

HOLT: What is that?

STIDHAM: That appears to be my notes from an interview with Mr. Misskelley on June 11, 1993.

HOLT: And we are back to where I wanted to get with the time records. On page three of the time records you have June 11, 1993 "conference with client." Would this in fact be the notes that you made during that conference?

STIDHAM: Yes, it would.

HOLT: Okay. And do you know when this got put in the file?

STIDHAM: I assume as soon as I got back to the office.

HOLT: So did you ever take it with you back to the jail?

STIDHAM: This particular statement?

HOLT: Yes?

STIDHAM: I have no idea. I just don't know.

HOLT: Okay. Do you know if that statement was ever reduced, uh, was ever put into a printed-type document?

STIDHAM: Not unless it's in that folder.

HOLT: I haven't been able to locate it.

STIDHAM: Then it wasn't, then.

HOLT: Okay. I can't really, uh, if you would, read what the I notes that you made with regard to that meeting that you had in those two and half hours with Mr. Misskelley?

STIDHAM: Do you want me to read the entire document?

HOLT: Yes, I do. Just to make sure —— you have good handwriting, but I can't make out every point.

STIDHAM: It' ll take a little time, but I'll see what I can do here. I made notes in paragraph form and paragraph one states that "seen picture of three b's," which was an abbreviation for boys.

HOLT: What was "C" in abbreviation?

STIDHAM: C?

HOLT: Was that your client?

STIDHAM: I'm not sure what "C" is — I'm sorry.

HOLT: Well, you started off, it says — seen pictures of three b's – oh, "seen picture of three b's about one week before murder" for instance, down on paragraph 3, I thought you were – we'll get to that.

STIDHAM: Okay. I'm sorry. I obviously wasn't speaking clearly enough.

Paragraph one: "Seen picture of three b's," which means 3 boys, **"one week before murder at cult meeting."** **Paragraph two: "At cult meeting he recognized three boys, but couldn't remember where he,"** horrible grammar, **"where he seen them until the picture was in paper."**

HOLT: Are you dictating this?

STIDHAM: No, I'm writing it as he is telling me.

HOLT: I mean, exactly, you're writing it as he is telling you.

STIDHAM: Well, to the best I can.

HOLT: Well, you wouldn't necessarily say "seen"?

STIDHAM: I don't have the best grammar in the world, so it's possible that that's my word instead of his.

HOLT: It's more likely that he in fact used the words "I seen"? That's common parlance among people who don't speak good English?

STIDHAM: It's possible. I think that says **"three teens were in water. Damien hollered at three boys, client," C,, which is short for client, "and Jason hid in weeds. Damien hit blonde-headed boy and then other two started hitting Damien." And the other two would be reference to other victims. "C, " being client, Mr. Misskelley, "and Jason came out and all started fighting."**
Paragraph 4 states that: "C," again referring to Mr. Misskelley, "started hitting boy in Scout uniform. J," which would be, uh, stand for Jason, "started hitting the other boy."
Paragraph 5: "Damien hit the blonde-headed boy with stick, unconscious, bleeding a little bit."
Paragraph 6: "Damien then went to Jason and other kid. Damien started hitting this boy and Jason went over to the blonde-

headed boy and stuck his dick into the boy's mouth."

Paragraph 7: "Client," it actually says 'C,' but it's obviously reference to the client, "kept hitting boy Scout and knocked him out unconscious, still breathing. C," being client, "was sure he was still breathing."

Paragraph 8: "The C," client, "went on to Damien and helped Damien hit the other boy."

And then it goes to page two. Paragraph 9: "Damien went to Boy Scout, pulled his pants down and screwed him in the ass."

Paragraph 10: "After Jason screwed blonde boy in the mouth, he screwed him in the butt. After he screwed him in the butt, he cut off blonde-headed boy's penis."

Paragraph 11: "After that, client realized it was time to stop. Client stopped hitting other kid. Client went over to Boy Scout, he was saying 'help us, help us.'"

Paragraph 12: "Client told Damien 'it's time to stop.' Damien said, 'No, we're going to,' —— I can't read my own writing.

HOLT: You're taking it down pretty fast weren't you?

STIDHAM: Yes, and of course, my handwriting is not the best. **It says, 'No, we're going to hide this,' or 'We're going to like this,' I think, is actually what it says. "Client helped Boy Scout up, Damien knocked client and boy down. Client told Damien and Jason to stop hurting boys."**
Paragraph 13: "Client walked away ten to fifteen feet and then came back."
Paragraph 14: "Damien screwed Boy Scout again. Jason stabbed one of the little boys in the face."
Paragraph 15: "Client and Damien and Jason tied all boys up with their own shoestrings. Client choked Boy Scout until he quit moving.
Paragraph 16: "All but the blonde was still alive. Client didn't choke blonde."
Paragraph 17: "Damien and Jason threw them in water. Saw boys kicking around in water."

Paragraph 18: "Client was afraid to go back and help, so he left."
And then the final page doesn't have any numbers with a paragraph. "No one ever mentioned killing anybody in cult. Damien would try to say voodoo stuff and try to," it says, "try to dogs, cats and snakes from the dead." I'm not sure exactly what that means. "Damien stuck his tongue in the skull of a bird." And that's the end of my notes.

HOLT: And you did, according to your practice, you testified the date — — what is the date on that?

STIDHAM: June 11, 1993.

On February 5, 1994, Misskelley was convicted by a jury of one count of first-degree murder in the case of Michael Moore and two counts of second-degree murder in the cases of Steven Branch and Christopher Byers. The court sentenced him to life plus 40 years in prison. His conviction was appealed and ultimately upheld by the Arkansas Supreme Court.

CHAPTER SEVEN
DAMIEN AND JASON AT
TRIAL

**Damien Echols and Jason Baldwin during
their trial in 1994**

Whenever you view any of the
documentaries or movies about the West
Memphis Three case, this is the part that
usually is so twisted and full of lies that it is
almost unbelievable to a person with any
common sense. When we decided to write
this book, we first sat down and viewed all

of the movies and read the books that talked about this case. Then after we actually had a chance to look at the evidence that the West Memphis Police and the State prosecutors office had, we were amazed at how inaccurate the books and movies had been. We noticed that each writer would put their own spin and twist on the facts to make them fit their own agenda. As a book author of true crime cases, I find it appalling that people would twist the facts and present them as truth in a book that they are marketing as non-fiction. When we first considered this case for a book, we all agreed that we would not put any spin on the information that we present as fact.

We know that people there will be some that are not going to accept what we write here as the truth. We also know that a lot of people have believed so many falsehoods on both sides of the issue that even when being presented with the real truth, it will be hard to accept.

We are going to present a lot of facts of this case that were not revealed in any of the West Memphis Three movements. These are the facts that many in the media did not want the public to see since it was in contradiction to their agenda. We are going to present the facts of the case and we will also provide you with the resource information that we used to obtain these facts. We are not doing this to prove innocence or guilt of any particular person or persons. Our ONLY goal is for the real truth to be revealed and that there will be justice for all the true victims involved, especially Michael, Stevie and Christopher.

Just two weeks after the guilty verdict in the Jessie Misskelley trial, jury selection began in a Jonesboro, Arkansas courtroom for the trial of Damien Echols and Jason Baldwin. The day before the trial opened, Dan Stidham made a public announcement, *"Mr. Misskelley made a decision last night that he is not going to testify against his codefendants."* The prosecutors knew that without Jessie's testimony, they were left with a very thin, circumstantial case. Fortunately for them, Judge Burnett denied a motion filed by Baldwin's attorneys asking that he be tried separately from Damien. Prosecutors knew that they had the right person on trial with Damien Echols. They knew that the evidence tying Echols to witchcraft, as well as some damaging statements by Damien and eye witnesses might lead a jury to a conclusion of "guilt by association" in Baldwin's case. The state was disappointed in the fact that they could not place the pick axe in Jason's hands on the night of the murders and that the evidence could not be presented in the trial. But they felt that the evidence that they did have and the eyewitnesses would be a sure bet for a guilty verdict.

On February 28th 1994, the trial began with opening statements from lead prosecutor John Fogleman. Fogleman told the jury that the state would prove "through scientific evidence" and "the statements of these own defendants" that "they caused the deaths of Michael Moore, Stevie Branch and Chris Byers." Jason Baldwin's attorney, Paul Ford, told the jury that Jason Baldwin, who was only sixteen at the time of his arrest, "is not a troublemaker." He took care "of his two younger brothers, getting them to bed. And in the morning, when Mom is still asleep because she's been up late, and it's Jason who has the obligation of getting himself up, getting his brothers up, getting everybody dressed and fed and catch the bus and go to school. That's the kind of person Jason Baldwin is." Ford also tried to show that his client was charged only because the West Memphis police department had completely disregarded statements given by witnesses and the physical evidence.

"You'll see that this evidence that they have...has been twisted and manipulated and distorted in order to make the pieces of the puzzle they want to build to fit together. And you'll see that from their own witnesses. Lastly, you will see from their own witnesses, evidence that will show that Jason Baldwin is innocent."

Finally, Scott Davidson, one of the attorneys for Damien Echols, gave his opening statement. Davidson knew that the jury would be thinking about Damien's past. He believed that some of the statements and actions of Damien in the past might affect the opinions of the jurors. So he made the decision to use his opening statement to address this concern from the very outset. Mr. Davidson told the jury that "He's not the all-American boy," and "He's kind of weird. He's not the same as maybe you and I might be...But I think you'll also see that there's simply no evidence that he murdered these three kids."

The State began making its case against Echols and Baldwin in pretty much the same way they had done in Jessie Misskelley's trial. They started with the parents of each child describing the last time they had seen their sons and the with the detectives describing how they had discovered the bodies of the three young boys and what other evidence they had found at the crime scene. The difference between the Echols and Baldwin trial from the trial of Jessie Misskelley, was alibi's that did not add up and an eyewitness placing Damien and Jason in the area of the killings on the night of the murders, May 5, 1993.

Below is a list of the alibis given by Damien Echols or his supporters that were shown to at best, have some holes, and at worst, shown to be outright lies.
Many years after the trial, in a 2010 interview with CNN, Damien made the following claims:

"At the time the police say the murders took place I was actually on the phone with three different people. The problem was, my attorneys never called them to the stand." - Damien Echols

If you search YouTube you can watch this interview. Below is the link to take you directly to it when you would like to view it on your own.

http://www.youtube.com/watch?v=leEtbjm2uHI#t=65s

There are four girls that Damien has claimed that he spoke with the evening of May 5th, 1993. If perhaps you are wondering why his attorneys did not call them to testify; here's why. It is because not a single one of them could account for his whereabouts from 5:30pm to 9:20pm on May 5th, 1993. The police and the medical examiner's office both believe that the murders occurred sometime between 6:45pm and 8:00 pm. In fact, some of the girls that Damien say are his alibis have made statements that actually place Damien WITH Jason Baldwin during that time. In fact, none of their statements would have provided alibis for Damien. To the contrary, they would have provided evidence that he was out of his home between 5:30pm and 9:20pm with Jason Baldwin on the night of May 5th, 1993.

They would have really made better prosecution witnesses than defense witnesses. Looking back now, Damien should be thankful they weren't called as witnesses in 1993. Because had they been called, they would have shed light on the fact that he really did not have an alibi for the night that the children were murdered. We discussed this in an earlier chapter also.

Here are summaries of the girls' police statements back in 1993 during the investigation:

Holly George: Damien claimed he talked to Holly George on May 5th, 1993. Holly told police that she did not talk to Damien that evening. She said she spoke with him much earlier in the afternoon, around 3:00pm or 4:00pm.

THIS IS DET. B. RIDGE OF THE WEST MEMPHIS POLICE DEPARTMENT, TODAY'S DATE 9/22/93. THE TIME IS 4:34 P.M. IN THE HOUSE WITH HOLLIE GEORGE AT ...WHAT IS THIS ADDRESS? HOLLIE- 5639 NORTH.

RIDGE- NORTH STREET IN BARTLETT, TENNESSEE. OKAY, HOLLIE THE QUESTIONS I NEED TO ASK YOU TODAY ...WE'VE ALREADY TALKED ONCE, UH, A COUPLE OF WEEKS AGO, AND HOW MANY TIMES DID YOU TALK TO DAMION ON THE 5TH OF MAY.

HOLLIE- ABOUT ONCE.

RIDGE- ONE TIME. AND WHAT TIME WAS THAT PHONE CONVERSATION?

HOLLIE- ABOUT 3 OR 4.

RIDGE- ABOUT WHAT TIME WOULD THAT BE?

HOLLIE- ABOUT 3:30 OR 4:00, SOMETHING LIKE THAT.

Heather Cliett: Damien claimed he spoke with Heather Cliett on the evening of May 5th, 1993. Cliett made a statement to the police and said that she had been unable to reach Echols until 10:30pm. She also mentioned that Holly George told her that Damien had been "out walking around" on May 5th, 1993.

She does not say that she was trying to call Damien. Her statement was that she was trying to call Jason. At no time in her statement does she say that she spoke with Damien during the day of May 5^{th,} 1993. She did say that she spoke to Damien at approximately 10:00 or 10:30 pm that night, but it was only for a few minutes.

Domini Teer: Damien's girlfriend, Domini Teer, said she last saw Damien around 5:00-5:30 pm on the evening of May 5th. She said she did not speak with him again until he called her around 10:00 pm that night.

One major issue in Domini's statement is the part where she says that she was at Jason's uncle's house with Jason, Ken and Damien while Jason mowed the lawn. Here is a portion of the statement she gave to the police about that day at Jason's uncle's house.

DOMINI- ME AND DAMION AND KEN, AND JASON MOWED THE LAWN, AND

WE ALL SAT WATCHING HIM FOR A LITTLE WHILE.

FOGLEMAN- DID YA'LL ALL MOW THE LAWN SOME.

DOMINI- NO, JUST JASON MOWED THE LAWN. WE ALL WATCHED.

FOGLEMAN- BUT YA'LL WATCHED.

DOMINI- YEAH.

FOGLEMAN- ALRIGHT. THEN WHAT HAPPENED?

DOMINI- WE SAT THERE FOR A WHILE WATCHING HIM MOW THE LAWN, AND THEN ME AND DAMION GOT UP AND WALKED TO THE LAUNDRYMAT...

FOGLEMAN- LET ME STOP YOU A

MINUTE BEFORE WE GET TO THE LAUNDRYMAT? UM...DID DAMION, EXCUSE ME, DID JASON GET THROUGH MOWING?

DOMINI- UH UH.

FOGLEMAN- DID YA'LL SEE ANYBODY THERE AT THE HOUSE? HIS UNCLE, OR?

DOMINI- HIS UNCLE.

FOGLEMAN- DID YOU SEE HIM? OKAY, DID YA'LL TALK TO HIM? BUT, YOU DID SEE HIM.

DOMINI- UH HUH.

FOGLEMAN- DID HE COME OUTSIDE?

DOMINI- YEAH.

FOGLEMAN- WHERE DID YA'LL SIT AND WATCH JASON?

DOMINI- ON THE BACK PORCH.

FOGLEMAN- AND WHERE WAS THE UNCLE?

DOMINI- GETTING THE LAWNMOWER OUT FOR JASON.

FOGLEMAN- AND WHERE WAS THE LAWNMOWER?

DOMINI- IN THE SHED.

FOGLEMAN- AND THE SHED IS IN THE BACK?

DOMINI- YEAH.

FOGLEMAN- OKAY, AND YA'LL WERE THERE ON THE BACK PORCH?

DOMINI- UH HUH.

According to Domini, she was sitting on the back porch with Damien and Ken watching Jason mow his uncle's yard. But when Jason's uncle was questioned about this, he stated that he did not see anyone at his home except for Jason.

Here is the statement that was made by Jason's uncle Hubert Bartoush regarding that day.

STATEMENT OF: Hubert B. Bartoush
DATE: PAGE:
1037 Park W. Mphs.
DOB: 10-3-29 S/R [omitted]

On 5-5-93 Jason Baldwin, my Grand Nephew, came to my house at about 4:30 PM and mowed my yard. He was alone when he was at my house. He left my house at about 6:30 PM and said he was going to Walmart to play video games. I remember the times because Jeopardy was coming on when he got here and Wheel of Fortune was coming on when he left.

When Domini was asked what time she left Jason's uncle's house and what she did for the remainder of the evening, this was her statement to the police.

FOGLEMAN- OKAY, AND HOW MUCH DID HE MOW BEFORE YA'LL GOT UP?

DOMINI- WELL, HE MOWED IN A CIRCLE AROUND THE YARD.

FOGLEMAN- UH HUH.

DOMINI- HE MOWED ABOUT LIKE, THREE CIRCLES, AND THEN WE ALL GOT UP AND LEFT.

FOGLEMAN- OK, YOU...

DOMINI- ME AND DAMION.

FOGLEMAN- WHAT ABOUT KEN?

DOMINI- HE STAYED THERE.

FOGLEMAN- WHERE DID JASON GO?

DOMINI- HE MOWED THE YARD.

FOGLEMAN- WHY DID YA'LL GET UP?

DOMINI- DAMION SAID HE HAD TO CALL HIS MOM.

FOGLEMAN- OKAY, WHY DID HE HAVE TO CALL HIS MOM?

DOMINI- TO COME PICK HIM UP. I DON'T KNOW, HE JUST CALLED HIS MOM.

FOGLEMAN- OKAY. WHAT DID YA'LL TALK ABOUT ON THE WAY FROM LAKESHORE TO JASON'S UNCLE'S

HOUSE?

DOMINI- ABOUT WHAT HAPPENED TO JASON AT SCHOOL, AND GOOFED OFF.

FOGLEMAN- NOTHING IN PARTICULAR.

DOMINI- NO.

FOGLEMAN- DID YA'LL TALK ABOUT ANY PLANS ABOUT WHAT YA'LL WERE GOING TO DO THAT NIGHT OR THE NEXT DAY?

DOMINI- NO.

FOGLEMAN- SO, YA'LL HAD PLANNED FOR THAT DAY, BUT YOU DIDN'T TALK ABOUT ANY PLANS FOR THE NEXT DAY, OR ANYTHING.

DOMINI- NO.

FOGLEMAN- AND YOU WENT TO THE LAUNDRYMAT?

DOMINI- UH HUH.

FOGLEMAN- AND WHAT DID YOU DO AT THE LAUNDRYMAT?

DOMINI- CALLED HIS MOM.

FOGLEMAN- OKAY, AND ABOUT WHAT TIME WAS THAT?

DOMINI- UM...PROBABLY ABOUT 5 OR 5:30, SOMETHING LIKE THAT.

FOGLEMAN- OKAY. THEN WHO CAME TO GET HIM?

DOMINI- HIS MOM AND HIS SISTER.

FOGLEMAN- HIS MOM AND HIS
SISTER?

DOMINI- UH HUH.

FOGLEMAN- ANYBODY ELSE?

DOMINI- I THINK HIS DAD WAS
THERE TOO.

FOGLEMAN- YOU DON'T REMEMBER?

DOMINI- YEAH, HIS DAD WAS THERE.

FOGLEMAN- ARE YOU SURE?

DOMINI- UH HUH. CAUSE HE WAS
DRIVING THE CAR.

FOGLEMAN- ALRIGHT AND THEY
PICKED YOU UP?

DOMINI- UH HUH.

FOGLEMAN- ALRIGHT, AND THEN
WHAT HAPPENED?

DOMINI- THEY TOOK ME HOME.

FOGLEMAN- ABOUT WHAT TIME DID
YOU GET HOME?

DOMINI- UM, AROUND, LIKE 5:45,
6:00. IN BETWEEN THERE.

FOGLEMAN- DO YOU REMEMBER
WHAT WAS ON T.V. WHEN YOU
CAME IN?

DOMINI- I DIDN'T LOOK AT THE T.V., I
WALKED THE DOG.

FOGLEMAN- OKAY, YOU JUST
WALKED IN AND WALKED THE DOG/

DOMINI- YEAH, I JUST CAME IN AND I

SAT AT THE KITCHEN TABLE JUST
FOR A COUPLE OF MINUTES, AND
THEN I GOT BORED, AND THEN I GOT
UP, GOT THE DOG'S LEASH AND
WALKED TO THE STORE WITH THE
DOG.

FOGLEMAN- HOW LONG DID YOU
WALK THE DOG?

DOMINI- OH, PROBABLY ABOUT 10
MINUTES.

FOGLEMAN- OKAY. AND THEN YOU
CAME BACK IN?

DOMINI- UH HUH.

FOGLEMAN- DO YOU REMEMBER
WHAT WAS ON WHEN YOU CAME
BACK IN AFTER WALKING THE DOG
FOR ABOUT 10 MINUTES?

DOMINI- UH HUH.

FOGLEMAN- WHAT?

DOMINI- CAUSE, TIMETRACKS WAS FIXIN TO COME ON.

FOGLEMAN- OKAY.

DOMINI- AND I TOOK A SHOWER, CAUSE MOM HAD TOLD ME WHAT HAPPENED WHILE TIMETRACKS ENDED. TIL THE END OF TIMETRACKS SHE HAD TOLD ME WHAT HAPPENED.

FOGLEMAN- OKAY, BUT IT WAS JUST COMING ON WHEN YOU CAME IN?

DOMINI- UH HUH.

FOGLEMAN- BUT, YOU DIDN'T WATCH IT? YOU TOOK A SHOWER,

ALRIGHT, THEN WHAT HAPPENED?

DOMINI- THEN I GOT OUT OF THE
SHOWER, AND I LAID IN BED FOR A
WHILE, AND DAMION CALLED, AND
ME AN HIM BICKERED BACK AND
FORTH FOR ALMOST AN HOUR, AND
THEN SHE MADE ME GET OFF THE
PHONE.

FOGLEMAN- WHAT TIME DID HE
CALL?

DOMINI- ABOUT 10.

Now when we look at these statements by
Domini and Mr. Bartoush, we can say that
maybe the time frames are off by a little bit.
But the police also interviewed Damien's
mother Pam Hutchison about the events of
that day.

We will focus on the phone call from Damien while he was at the Laundromat and the time frame involved in this portion of Pam's statement.

RIDGE: OKAY, WHAT DID YOU DO FOR THE REST OF THE DAY?

HUTCHISON: WELL, I WENT HOME AND GOT READY TO COOK AND ABOUT I WOULD SAY AROUND 3:45, DAMIEN CALLED ME AND ASKED ME TO COME AND GET HIM, AND HE WAS AT THE LAUNDRY MAT ON MISSOURI STREET WITH DOMINI, JASON HAD TO MOW, I BELIEVE IT WAS HIS UNCLE'S YARD, THAT AFTERNOON, SO HE DIDN'T GET TO SPEND ANY TIME WITH DAMIEN, CAUSE HE HAD TO GO AND MOW THAT

HUTCHISON: (CON'T) YARD, SO I WENT AND PICKED HIM UP, ALONG

WITH DOMINI. I CARRIED DOMINI BACK TO HER TRAILER AND BROUGHT DAMIEN HOME WITH ME. WE WERE AT THE TRAILER BY 4 O'CLOCK.

RIDGE: BY 4 O'CLOCK

HUTCHISON: UM, UM

RIDGE: ALRIGHT, DO YOU KNOW WHERE JASON'S UNCLE LIVES?

HUTCHISON: UH, IT'S A STREET BEHIND GRANNY'S FRONT PORCH, THE RESTAURANT.

RIDGE: OKAY, WOULD IT BE ON THAT STREET THAT RUNS BY GRANNY'S FRONT PORCH?

HUTCHISON: THE ONE THAT RUNS RIGHT BEHIND IT

RIDGE: NORTH AND SOUTH?

HUTCHISON:

SUDBURY: PARK STREET, COULD IT BE PARK

HUTCHISON: I DON'T EVEN KNOW THE NAME OF IT WAS, YOU JUST GO BY GRANNY'S FRONT PORCH AND IT'S THE FIRST STREET.

SUDBURY: TO THE LEFT

HUTCHISON: RIGHT, TO THE RIGHT

SUDBURY: YOU COME OFF MISSOURI STREET, YOU GO IN FRONT OF GRANNY'S AND THEN TAKE A RIGHT, AND THAT IS PARK STREET.

HUTCHISON: OKAY

RIDGE: UH, AFTER DAMIEN WAS AT HOME, DID YOU SEE JASON?

HUTCHISON: NO. I DID NOT

RIDGE: ALRIGHT, SO IT WAS JUST DAMIEN AND DOMINI THAT YOU PICKED UP?

HUTCHISON: RIGHT

RIDGE: ALEXANDER'S LAUNDRY?

HUTCHISON: RIGHT

RIDGE: OKAY, AND THIS IS ABOUT 3:45?

HUTCHISON: UH, UH,

RIDGE: AND YOU TOOK HER HOME?

HUTCHISON: AND I TOOK HIM HOME WITH ME.

RIDGE: YOU TOOK HIM HOME WITH YOU? AND ABOUT WHAT TIME DID YOU GET HOME?

HUTCHISON: IT WAS ABOUT TEN [?] MINUTES AFTER FOUR, CAUSE I JUST WENT STRAIGHT TO LAKESHORE AND OUT, AND CAME RIGHT STRAIGHT HOME.

Now according to Pam, she received the phone call from Damien at approximately 3:45 pm to pick him and Domini up at the Laundromat. Then she stated that she was back at home with Damien by 4:10 pm.

Jason's uncle stated that Jason did not arrive at his house until approximately 4:30 pm. This would have been the time frame that Damien and Domini were already home according to Pam's statement. So, if we take the fact that Jason's uncle can specify his time frame according to the TV show schedules that were playing when Jason arrived and left his home,and if we can take what Pam gave as a statement as being the truth, then that would support the idea that Damien and Domini were in fact never at Jason's uncle's house as they had stated.

Now we return to another statement given by another girl that Damien spoke with on the night of May 5, 1993.

Jennifer Bearden: Bearden told police in a statement on 9/10/93 that she called Jason's house between 4:15 pm and 5:30 pm on the evening of May 5th, 1993. She said that Jason answered the phone and she talked to both Jason and Damien for about 20 minutes. She stated that Damien told her that he and Jason were "going somewhere" and asked her to call him back later that evening around 8:00 pm. When Bearden tried calling Damien's house at 8:00 pm, his grandmother answered. Damien's grandmother told Bearden that Damien "wasn't there." In her statement to the police, Bearden said that she was finally able to reach Damien at approximately 9:20 pm.

This is her statement concerning that time frame.

RIDGE: About what time was that call you made to Jason's?
BEARDEN: Between, it had to be somewhere in between 4:15 and 5, something like that 5, 5:30
RIDGE: Who answered the phone at Jason's?
BEARDEN: Jason
RIDGE: And did you talk to Damien?
BEARDEN: Yeah I talked to Jason about 5 minutes and the (inaudible) with Damien and he wasn't talking because they were playing video games with his little brother

Matt

RIDGE: Okay, and after that conversation you had with him

BEARDEN: He said him and Jason were going to go somewhere, him and Jason were going somewhere and that he, um, wanted me to call him later at his house around 8 and I said okay.

RIDGE: Okay, did he say where he was going to go?

BEARDEN: No.

RIDGE: Okay, and when you called back about 8.

BEARDEN: His Grandmother said he wasn't there, and I was suppose to call back around 9, and I called back around 9:20, 9:30 and I talk to him for a little bit, but then I had to get off the phone, because I wasn't suppose to be on the phone after 9:30.

During her conversation with Damien around 9:20 pm, Bearden stated that Damien told her he had been "out" with Jason. He claimed that they had been driven somewhere by Jason's mother, Angela Gail Grinnell.

RIDGE: Okay, after that last call and you talked to Damien, did you ask him where he had been that evening?
BEARDEN: I said where did you and Jason go, and he said, uh, his Mom just took us some where, he didn't really say where, because like -
RIDGE: Who's Mom took him somewhere?
BEARDEN: Jason's

What Damien did not take into consideration was the fact that Jason's mother could not have driven them anywhere because she was at work from 3:00 pm until 11:00 pm on the night of May 5th, 1993.

Here is a portion of the statement given to the police by Jason Baldwin's mother, Angela Grinnell.

FOGLEMAN: OKAY, WHAT HOURS DO YOU WORK THERE? ANGELA: I WORK FROM 3 TO 11.

She even goes on in her statement to say that Jason was asleep when she came home that evening.

*(Note) *When you read the statement made by Bearden, she also mentions a necklace that she had given to Jason. She makes the following statement regarding the necklace. **

RIDGE: OKAY, DID YOU KNOW JESSIE?

JENNIFER: YEA, I DIDN'T LIKE HIM THOUGH, BUT THE THING IS EVERYBODY SAYS THEY WERE FRIENDS, BUT THEY WERE NOT FRIENDS.

RIDGE: JESSIE, DAMIEN, AND JASON WERE NOT FRIENDS?

JENNIFER: NO, UN UN (NO) BECAUSE I LET JASON HAVE ONE OF MY NECKLACES

RIDGE: OKAY

JENNIFER: AND JESSIE STOLE IT FROM THEM AND UH, DAMIEN AND JASON DID NOT LIKE HIM FOR THAT REASON AND BECAUSE JESSIE REALLY HAD A BAD ATTITUDE HE WAS LIKE, HE HAD HE THINK, HE THOUGHT HE COULD BEAT UP EVERYBODY.

RIDGE: UM UM (YES)

JENNIFER: HE HAD STOLE THE 8 BALL FROM THE SKATE WORLD HE WAS WALKING AROUND WITH IT THEY HAD THOUGHT DAMIEN HAD STOLE IT, BUT IT WAS REALLY JESSIE, BECAUSE JESSIE WALKED TO ME AND HE HAD IT.

So when we look at the alibi witnesses that Damien provided, we know a couple of things for sure.

#1 He was not at Jason's uncle's house at the time that Jason was there to mow the lawn. This statement was contradicted by statements made by Jason's Uncle and Damien's mother.

#2 Not a single one of Damien's alibi witnesses could account for his whereabouts from 5:30 pm to 9:20 pm on May 5th, 1993. The police and the medical examiner's office both believe that the murders occurred between 6:45pm and 8:00 pm.

#3 By Damien's own admission, he was in fact with Jason Baldwin during the time frame in which the murders took place.

#4 Damien lied when he stated that he was out with Jason being driven by Jason's mother.

The statements given by these girls only verify that Damien and Jason were not at home during the time of murders. They also place the two of them together during this time frame. (By Damien's own admission to Jennifer Bearden).

Some people will poingt out that this does not place Damien and Jason in the area of Robin Hood Hills at the time that the murders took place. We agree that none of the statements made by any of these girls places Damien, Domini or Jason in the area of the killings.

But, what does place them near the crime scene the night of May 5, 1993, is a statement given by Narlene Hollingsworth who knew Domini personally. She gave a statement to the police that she saw both Domini and Damien in the area of Robin Hood Hills at the time of the killings. Here is the statement that Narlene gave to the West Memphis Police regarding what and who she saw that night.

STATEMENT OF Narlene Hollingsworth
203 Sycamore, Lakeshore
Date: 5-10-93

DABBS: This is Det. Dabbs and Lt. Diane
Hester. This is Monday, 05/10/93, 4:20. We
are talking to Narlene Hollingsworth at 203
Sycamore, telephone number, 735-xxxx in
reference to information she is giving us on
what she saw on a Damian subject and a L.
G. Hollingsworth.

HESTER: Narlene, just start with Monday,
last Wednesday, when you said that you had
picked up L. G., just start from when you
picked him up and go from there.

NARLENE: Okay, L.G., I was suppose to
have picked L. G. Hollingsworth up at
home

HESTER: Which is

NARLENE: Wednesday morning *(note from author "Wednesday" is May 5th 1993 the day of the murders)*

HESTER: And that's

NARLENE: He come to my house about 9:00 and we left from there looking for him

HESTER: That in the morning?

NARLENE: Right, so then we found the job and we went back home, and he said that he had to be home by 4:30, so he kept on around my home saying that he wanted to go home, so I said, okay. So, it was between 20 after 5, yeah it was 20 after 4 and we left my house. I took him straight to McAuley where he live.

HESTER: Alright we just drove by that address it was 714 McAuley Circle, is that correct?

NARLENE: 714 McAuley Circle, okay then I left him. And the street I took lead me straight down to Weaver School,

DABBS: And that was on McAuley Cirlce back to Holiday Drive?

NARLENE: Right,

DABBS: Then back south on Wilson, to E. Barton

NARLENE: Uh, uh

DABBS: Which you took a right and you went back west on Barton.

NARLENE: Right, and that's when I seen the three little boys on the bicycles.

HESTER: Alright, describe these boys that you saw.

DABBS: Where were they at when you saw them?

NARLENE: Okay, they were just before you get to Weaver School. And, then they were going so fast on that bicycle, and then one of them come out in front of me and I honked at him and told him that he needed to get out of the street. You know, before he get run over.

HESTER: Describe these boys that you saw.

NARLENE: Okay, there was two smaller boys and a little heavy set boy, a little heavier than the rest of them. And the little heavy set one had little bit darker hair than the rest of them. If I am not mistaken, the little heavy set boy had on a pair of green shorts with some black in it, with black and white tennis shoes on. But, I think they all three were wearing shorts, but I am not really sure about the other two, because I go a good look at the little dark headed boy. That's the one that I can really describe better than the rest.

HESTER: Okay, were they all three on bikes?

NARLENE: They were all three on bicycles, yes they were. And nice bicycles.

HESTER: What did the bicycles look like?

NARLENE: Well, one had look like some black in it, and I believe one of them had some light green in it, if I'm not mistaken. But, all three of those boys were together, two in front and one in the back. And they were flying on them bicycles. And, I told them little boys you ought to go home and that little boy said, no we are going to play for a little while. So, they were headed, what is the street

HESTER: This is Barton

NARLENE: Down Barton, they were headed away from their homes and cause I know that the live back the other way, because Sheila, the lady that live in the apartments told me that they did live back the other way, when spoke to her. So, they were going away from their homes. I never saw them little boys again, but Idid see uhh something later on Wednesday night.

HESTER: Okay, did you go home?

NARLENE: Did I go straight home?

HESTER: After this?

NARLENE: Yes, I did, I went straight to my house and cooked a do what I always do when, okay, what happened was Dixie

Hollingsworth had asked me to pick her up at where she works at a laundry mat, she said, will you pick me up, I get off at 10, I said, yes I will.

HESTER: Alright, where is the laundry mat?

NARLENE: That laundry mat is right there on Ingram. Okay

DABBS: Is that the one next to the Flash Market?

NARLENE: Yes it is, it's right there.

DABBS: Okay

NARLENE: Okay, I got ready to go, and my husband went with me and my children were too. And, on our way, coming do[wn] like you're going to Love's, I saw Dominic and Damia[n] coming down the street.

DABBS: What time was this?

NARLENE: This was exactly 20minutes til 10, exactly, cause w[e] had our watches and we knew what time it was. Okay they had dark clothing on and they were not cleaned.

DABBS: You said at one time that they were muddy all over.

NARLENE: They did have dirt on them, yes they did, now

HESTER: Now, which way were they walking?

NARLENE: They was coming back towards Lakeshore, this way.

DABBS: Okay, they were headed back uh, west, as you were goi[ng] east on the Service Road (South)

NARLENE:Right

DABBS: They were walking back west and you said that they were by a yellow marker?

NARLENE: They were, it was a yellow uh, sign thing up in, so[me] stick standing up and then they were just before th[ey] [or that] got to there, where they was.

DABBS[IMAGE STATES DABBS BUT SHOULD BE NARLENE]: Okay, as we were driving by, she pointed the stick [over] [or out] to us, and it's right there on the off ramp, where [?] Street as you go east down the interstate, the off ramp off to the South Service Road, is where the yellow stick or marker was.

HESTER: And they would have been on the south side.

DABBS: And they were on the south side of the South Service Road headed west, against the traffic, okay.

NARLENE: Okay, from then I don't know.

DABBS: Who all was with you when you saw these

NARLENE: Tabitha Hollingsworth, Ricky Hollingsworth, and uh, I believe Mary Hollingsworth and Little Ricky Hollingsworth was in the car too. I think all of us was in that car together that night.

HESTER: Are these all your children?

NARLENE: They sure is, my whole family.

DABBS: Your husband and your children?

NARLENE: Right

DABBS: Okay

NARLENE: And I

DABBS: Didn't you say that you also uh, saw, had your, were you driving?

NARLENE: Uh, yeah

DABBS: And you said that you turned your bright lights on wh[en]

you saw them, so that you could definitely see them?

NARLENE: So, that I could get a good look at them, to see who they were, yes I did. And I said, that's Dominic and Damian, no don't look like, it is and I got a good close look and said, it sure is.

HESTER: Alright, these people are known

to you, is that corre[ct]

NARLENE: Ma'am

HESTER: These people are known to you, Dominic and Damian?

NARLENE: Yes, I see them all the time

HESTER: How long have you known them?

NARLENE: Well, I don't really know Damian, cause I don't go around him from all the bad things that I hear about him, but therefore, I don't let my children go around him and Dominic, I've known her all of her life. Cause I use to hold her on my hip when she was six months old baby.

DABBS: You did advise that she lives behind trailer there?

NARLENE: Yes, she does

DABBS: At his time?

NARLENE: She lives in my sister's trailer,
Pamela Hollingsworth

DABBS: Okay, what did you do then, right
after you saw them?

NARLENE: Well, I was upset about it, for
them being out that late and around that
area, but you know I was wondering what
theywere doing out at that time of the night.
My husband told me to quit worrying about
it, cause they are out all the time. He said
that he sees them all the time. So, he told me
to quit worrying about it. So, then when I
talked to Dixie Hollingsworth, I got to the
laundry mat, she said that L. G.
Hollingsworth had just left from there in
some car. And, I said uh, that's funny, she
said that it i[s] and she never did say why,

and I thought it was funny, but I thought that he had just left from there and they were coming down the street. So, then when I talked to Dixie about it, I told Dixie what I had seen and she

said, yeah that is kinda odd. I said, yeah it is, I said Dixie, those little children and later on they found out that they were dead, I said Dixie that's kinda odd for them to be out that time of night and those little kids were dead, don't you think, she said yes I do, yes I do. I said, let me ask you something, I said since you know Damian better than me, do you think that he's capable of anything like that and she said, yes, I do. She said because he's in with the devil.

Unfortunately there are not a lot of detailed locations in Narlene's statement. We do know the location of Narlene's house and we know the location of The Flash market located on Ingram. So when we look at the most obvious route that Narlene would have taken that night we can create a map of the area.

We do know that they were spotted near an off-ramp to the South Service Road, as you go east down the interstate. This would of put them within walking distance to the crime scene.

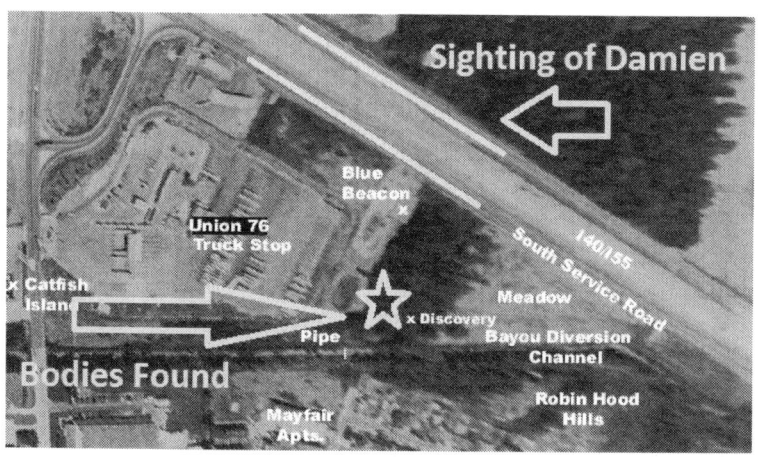

View of the crime scene area with the South service road marked

The other evidence that was collected in this case was sticks that were believed to have been used in the commission of the crime. Unfortunately the information about sticks being used in the process of killing the kids did not come to light until the police talked with Jessie. And by the time that Detective Rid went back to the crime scene in search of the sticks almost two months had passed.

While Detective Bryn Ridge was responding to a question on cross-examination about a delay of two months in retrieving the sticks and entering them into evidence, he said, "I didn't take that stick into evidence until the statement of Jesse Misskelley, in which he said--", the defense team immediately asked for a mistrial. They insisted that "blurting out the fact that Jesse Misskelley gave a confession" was extremely prejudicial and unwarranted by his question, but Judge Burnett was unmoved. "There isn't a soul up on that jury or in this courtroom that doesn't know Mr. Misskelley gave a statement," the judge said, explaining his decision to deny the motion.

Ridge also testified, that during Damien's long interrogation at the police station he had claimed all persons hold "demonic forces inside them," made observations about the mystical significance of water, and noted that three--the number of boys killed, of course--was "a sacred number in the

Wicca religion." Ridge also testified, Damien acknowledged reading books by Stephen King, an author famous for his horror novels--a fact Ridge thought was "strange."

To further develop his theme of a cult-related motive, Fogleman called Deanna Holcomb, Damien's former girlfriend, to tell jurors that Damien "wore all black" and that he always carried knives, sometimes in his trench coat pocket. An officer who conducted a search of Damien's home also testified that the search turned up eleven black T-shirts, the book *Never on a Broomstick*, and the skull of a dog. The prosecutor also asked Judge Burnett to take "judicial notice that there was a full moon on May 5, according to the almanac"—this was a request the judge found "appropriate."

To prove pre-meditation and motive for Jason and Damien's trial, the State called on the testimony of Dr. Dale Griffis, a "cult expert" from Ohio. The testimony concerning the occult took center stage with the calling of Dr. Griffis. Griffis had received his doctorate from Columbia Pacific University in 1984 after studying by correspondence for four years. Since that time he had proclaimed himself as a "Cult-Cop" and gave lectures and seminars on the dangers of adolescent involvement in satanic activities. It is difficult to determine his qualification for the term "expert," as according to the F.B.I there is very little evidence to substantiate stories about satanic ritual murders in the United States.

It seems that Judge Burnett, while questioning the validity of the discipline of social psychology as studied by Dr. Richard Ofshe, an expert on false confessions and police coercion and Professor of Sociology at UC Berkeley, did not have any problems with the rather dubious credentials of Dr. Griffis and allowed his testimony to be admitted.

Griffis testified that the number three was "one of the most powerful numbers in the practice of satanic belief." When he was asked on cross-examination whether the number three might also have any special significance in the Christian belief system (consider, for example, the Trinity), Griffis said, "I cannot make that statement." Griffis said that the murderers of the three boys "were using the trappings of occultism during this event," pointing to "the time of the moon phase" and "the removal of blood" as examples of "trappings." When he was asked what significance the sucking of blood might have, Griffis explained, "Blood is the life force. And usually they will take--they prefer to have a child that is young, very young, and the younger, the more innocent, the better the life force."

Some of the testimony of Dr. Griffis was later determined to be unproven or false. Even though Damien did in fact have an interest in the occult and studied the religion it was determined later that Dr. Griffis made statements concerning this crime that was not 100% accurate and in some cases they were just his personal opinions.

The basis of his testimony was that the crime scene "Bore the trappings of occultism." In his opinion, the most obvious points in this crime which suggested to him that the murders were Satanic in nature were:

He noted that these killings were carried out on a date close to a pagan holiday and on a full moon.

There is a Neo-Pagan festival held on the first of May, known as Beltane. Beltane is the Gaelic May Day festival. Most commonly it is held on April 30th, but sometimes on May 1st, or about halfway between the spring equinox and the summer solstice. It is only celebrated on that day, not four days later. We will also note that bonfires are part of the ritual of this holiday and there was no evidence of a bonfire at the scene of the murders. And we have not found any references to sacrifices being part of the Beltane holiday rituals. We also discovered that Satanists do not hold rituals only on a full or new moon. Most of these beliefs came from the movie industry that portrayed the full moon as a time of rituals and sacrifices for satin worshiper.

He also stated that young children were often sought for sacrifice because they provided a "better... life force."

We have found no evidence that any children have been ritually murdered in the past century in the United States by the followers of any religion. But we will say that there have been cases where people have been killed as sacrifices by people who claimed to have been following the satanic religion. This is mainly done due to the fact that many people follow the popular movie depicted version of satin worshiping instead of actually studying the true beliefs of the religion.

When we spoke to true followers of the satanic religion they informed us that the more common followers of Satanism are young kids who want to mold their lifestyle to the lyrics of their favorite heavy metal bands. And by doing so, they start to believe that the songs are a true definition of satin worshiping. These "followers" are uneducated and tend to commit numerous killings in the name of their "religion".

He also stated that the age of the victims reflected the significance of the number eight as a witch's number.

There are a couple of issues with this statement. First of all it was proven that this was not a planned or calculated murder. The fact that the three boys were not stalked or lured to the murder location proves that this was just a crime of opportunity. And because this was a crime of opportunity there is no significance to the exact ages of the children. It is merely a coincidence of the ages. And the number eight has no significance in the Wiccan or any other pagan religions.

The number of victims reflected the significance of the number three in occultism.

The only reference to the number three that was ever tied to any pagan religion was a brief mentioning of the significance when we researched areas concerning witchcraft. This is their beliefs when it deals with the number three.

The spiritual meaning of number Three deals with magic, intuition, fecundity, and advantage. The number Three invokes expression, versatility, and pure joy of creativity. Three is also a time identifier as it represents Past, Present and Future. Consecutive Threes in your life may symbolize the need to express yourself creatively, or consider your present directional path in relation to past events and future goals. Three may also represent promising new adventures, and assurance of cooperation from others whom you may require help. Three typically symbolizes reward and success in most undertakings.

Actually we discovered that Christianity places more significance on this number because of its belief in a Triune God (the Father, Son and Holy Spirit).

The manner in which the victims were tied was significant as being tied ankle to wrist exposed the genitalia. And that the removal of Christopher Byers's testicles was significant as they are removed in satanic rituals for the semen.

The statement regarding the collection of semen from the testicles has two major flaws in it. In high school biology we learned that semen is not stored in the testicles. And the 2nd and probably the most important part of this statement is the fact that a male does not produce semen at all until adolescence.

Dr. Griffis claimed that the absence of blood at the scene was significant because due to the fact that cult members often store blood for future uses. It is believed that they would either drink or bathe in the blood.

It has been believed since the 16th century that Satanists drink or bathe in human blood. Though it is often mentioned in folklore and portrayed in the movies it has never been part of any satanic rituals.

Most younger and uneducated followers of their own satanic religion like to interchange the folklore of vampires and witches into their own made up beliefs. By doing this they create an image of a fantasy world where they put themselves in a fantasy world with witches from fairytales and to some extent even Bram Stoker's fictional Count Dracula.

He also believed that the cleared area found on the bank could be consistent with a ritual or a satanic ceremony.

In order for this statement to hold any validity we would have to of found other clues to support this. It would be expected that in the case of a Satanic ritual there would be evidence of other ritual tools, such as an altar, a circle on the ground or evidence of a fire.

It was also believed that sacrifices were often performed near water for a baptism-type ritual or just to wash the blood away.

Baptism is a Christian ritual which is not shared by any pagan religions and certainly not Satanists. And as for the crime being committed near water: It is due to the fact that this was only a crime of opportunity.

During the cross-examination, Dr. Griffis stated that if he had been asked by the State to testify to conditions opposite to the conditions described it could still be related to satanic activity. He also stated that his original testimony had not included the blood traits. He had included them only after learning that morning, that Michael Carson would be testifying that Jason Baldwin had confessed to sucking blood from Christopher Byers's penis.

Dr. Griffis's testimony supported the many myths and fears surrounding witchcraft and Satanism which were widely known by the West Memphis community already. Dr. Griffis's words spoke deeply to the superstitions and fears of the jury and any attempt to refute them would probably have fallen on deaf ears.

Well let's start with the Lake Knife. A knife was found submerged blade down in the pond directly behind Jason Baldwin's home by Officer Joel Mullins on November 17, 1993.

Discovery of the Lake Knife by Officer Joel
Mullins

Damien's ex-girlfriend, Deanna Holcomb,
testified during the trial that the knife was
similar to a knife that belonged to Damien.
She said Damien's knife was unique because
it had a compass on the end. During the trial,
a knife distributor testified that the lake
knife had a missing compass.

Unfortunately for the prosecutors not only
did Damien own a similar knife that was
found in the lake, but so did numerous other
people. After the movie Rambo was released

there were numerous knives sold on the market known as "Rambo Knives".

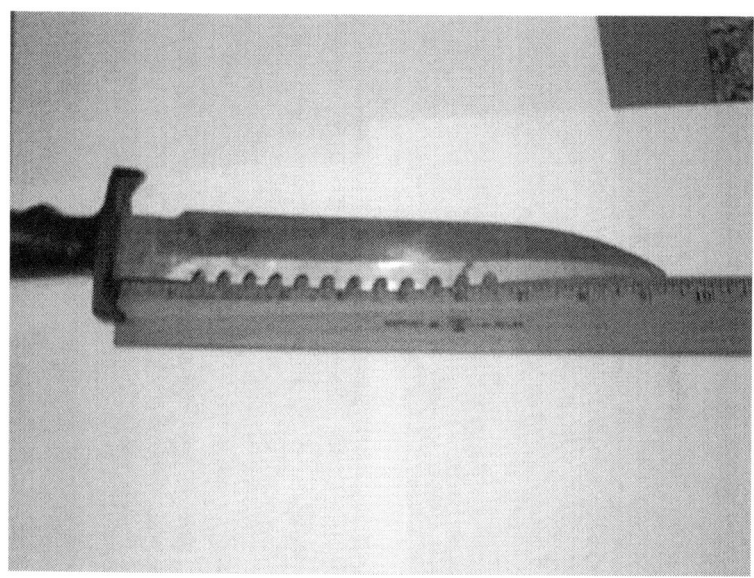

Here is the actual knife that was found in the lake behind Jason Baldwin's home

Here are the partial transcripts of Deanna Holcomb's testimony during the trial when she testifies about Damien owning a similar knife as the one found in the lake.

Fogleman: Ok. Now during the time that you uh - went with him, did Damien carry any type of weapon?

Holcomb: Knives.

Fogleman: Pardon?

Holcomb: Knives.

Fogleman: Ok. I want to show you what has been introduced as exhibit 77 and ask if you've seen a knife like that before?

Holcomb: Yes sir.

Fogleman: Alright. Where did you see it and under what circumstances?

Holcomb: Uh - I saw it in his coat pocket. His lea - his trench coat pocket.

Fogleman: Alright, how did you see it in his coat pocket?

Holcomb: Um - I went to hu - put my arm around his waist and it was there.

Fogleman: Alright. Did - well, did you uh - how did you - what did you do after you found it there?

Holcomb: I took it out to look at it.

Fogleman: Ok. And it was - was it a knife like that?

Holcomb: Similar, yes sir.

Fogleman: Alright. What was - what if anything was different about the knife that you pulled out of Damien's pocket?

Holcomb: It had a compass on the end.

Fogleman: On the end, ok. You're talking about right here?

Holcomb: Yes sir.

Fogleman: I don't know if the jury saw that - would you point to the area where the compass was?

Holcomb: Right there.

Fogleman: Now, could you identify the

person that you've - that you said uh - had a knife like that?

Holcomb: Yes sir.

Fogleman: Is he in the courtroom?

Holcomb: Yes sir.

Fogleman: Would you point him out for the jury?

Holcomb: Right there.

Fogleman: Which one?

Holcomb: The one in the black sweater.

Fogleman: Your Honor, may the record reflect the witness has identified the defendant?

The Court: It may so reflect.

(mumbling about cameras)

The Court: Yeah.

Fogleman: I don't have any further questions at this time, your Honor.

After Deana was finished with her testimony James Parker was called to testify regarding the knife. Mr. Parker operated a knife company in Chattanooga, Tennessee that sold knives similar to the one that the police had found.

All Mr. Parker was able to testify is that there was in fact a compass on the handle of the knife and that there were allot of these knives manufactured and distributed in the mid 1980's.

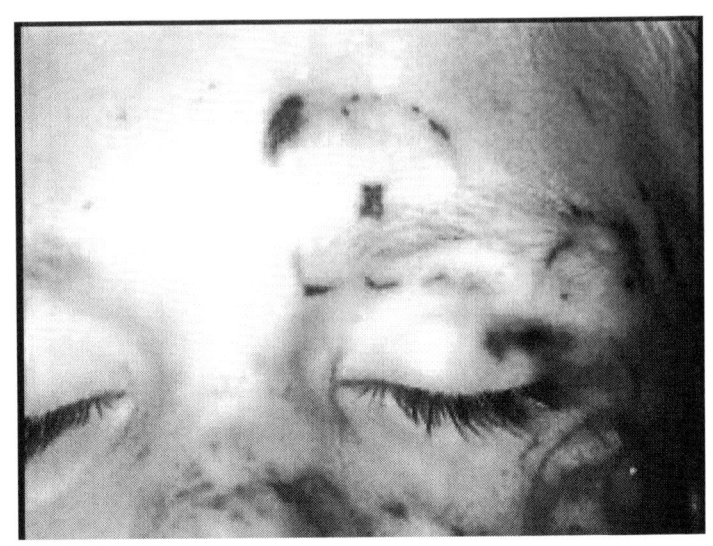

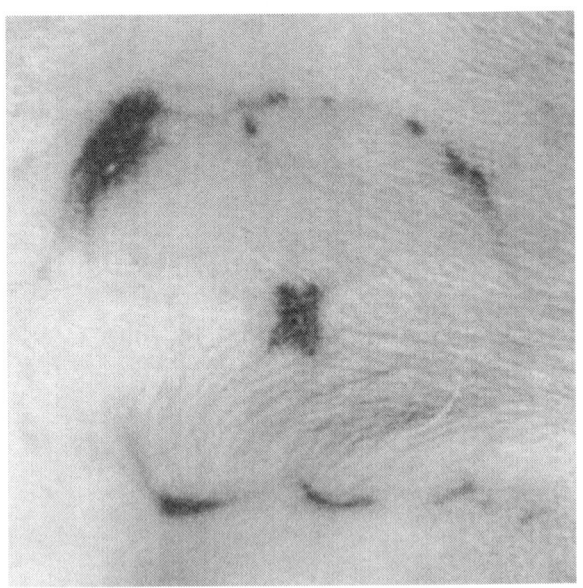

The wound found on the face of Steven
Branch

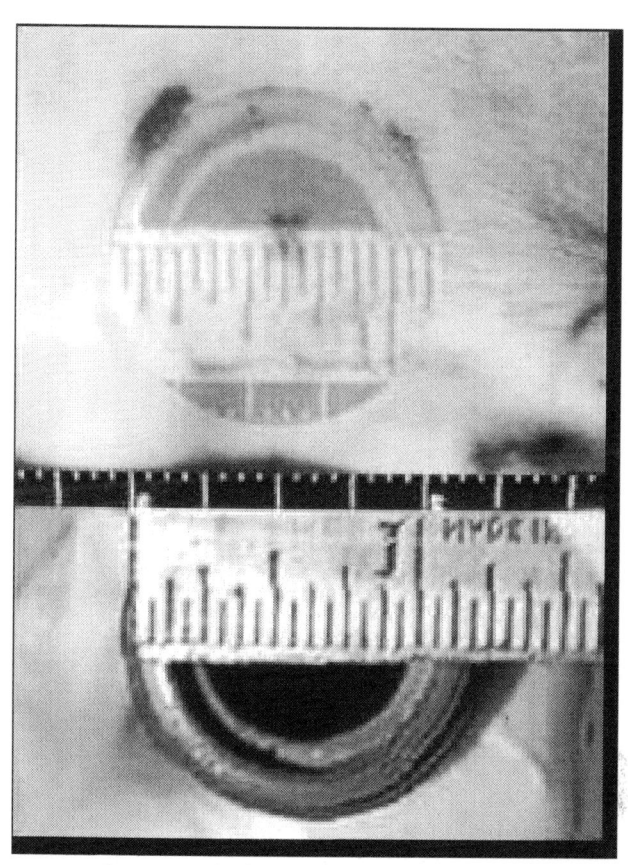

Comparison of the wound size verses the
size of the knife end

This is what the knife may have looked like
before the compass was removed

Year after the trials, a veteran West
Memphis Three case researcher revisited
what had been described as a human bite
mark on Stevie Branch's forehead. The
researcher had two forensics experts
compare the wound to the missing compass
slot on the handle of the lake knife. The
forensics experts found that the round slot
where the compass had been matched the

wound on Branch's forehead. In addition, the "X" mark in the center of Branch's forehead wound was similar to the peg in the hole where the compass had been.

Many West Memphis Three supporters claim that the marks on Stevie's forehead are human bite marks. What they fail to acknowledge is the size and pattern of the wounds.

We discussed this wound with a Forensic Odontology expert who specializes in bite-mark evidence. The expert pointed out a couple of things that made a lot of sense. The child was 8 years old so the eyebrow is not very long. And the mark goes from the "INSIDE" of the bridge of the nose to 1/3 (at the most) down the length of the eyebrow. The only way that this could be a bite mark is if it was made by an infant because adult human bite patterns would be at least twice this length. He also noted that there is not an adult human alive today or ever for that matter, that would leave a perfect circular bite pattern only 1 inch wide. All human teeth are in the shape closely resembling oval not circular. So much for the bite mark theory that so many West Memphis Three supporters are building their case on.

The second part of the knife theory has to do with scratches found on the boys. Prosecutors believed that the scratches came from the serrated side of the knife found in the lake.

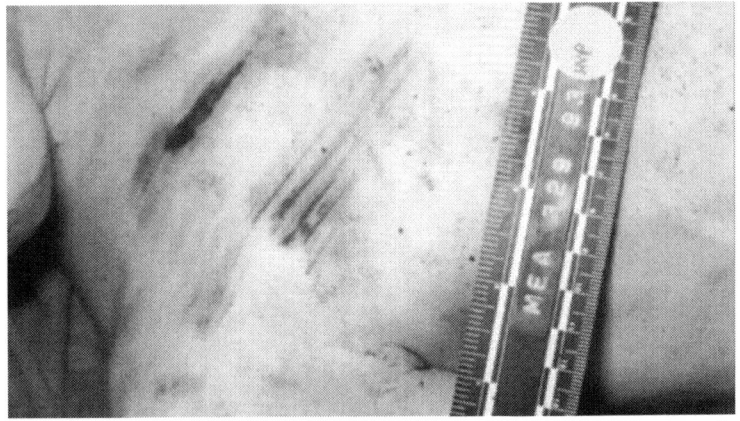

Scratches found on one of the victim's body

The problem with this theory is the consistency of the scratches. If the scratches actually came from the serrated side of the knife found the scratches would be more uniformed and consistent. Here is another look at the knife.

Let's focus on the spacing between the serrated sections of the knife blade. You can plainly see that the spacing on the knife and the spacing on the victim is not consistent. Also with the knife the area of the wound would be approximately the same length of the serrated section of the knife. You can see the size of the wound on the victim does not match the size of the serrated section of the knife. (The serrated side of the knife is approximately 6 inches long and the scratches on the body are nowhere near that length)

We will also note that the scratches on the victim would all be very close in depth and length had the knife actually been used. We can clearly see many variances in the wound pattern on the body.

Later on after the trials it was believed that the scratches on the body of Steven Branch did not come from the knife found in the lake. But it was believed that they came from turtles living in the water were the bodies had been found.

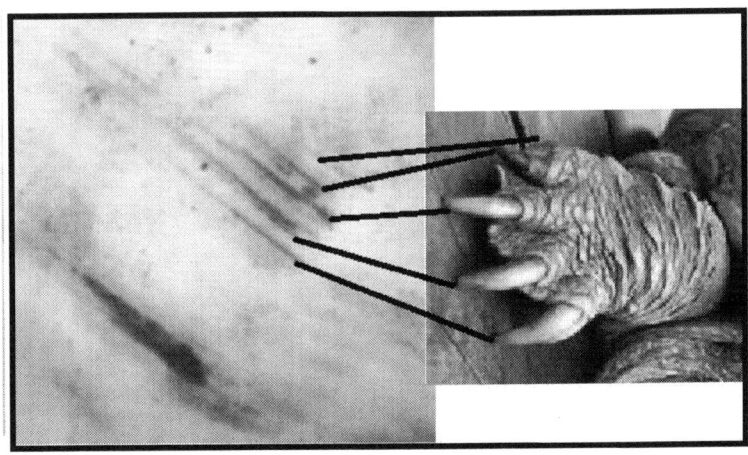

Here is a side by side comparison

Could this be the explanation for the scratches found on the bodies? Most people who investigated this theory believe that the scratches found on the bodies were more than likely caused by turtles. Several bite marks that were attributed to turtles where found on the bodies. We would also like to note that the area that the bodies were found in is known as "Turtle Hill."

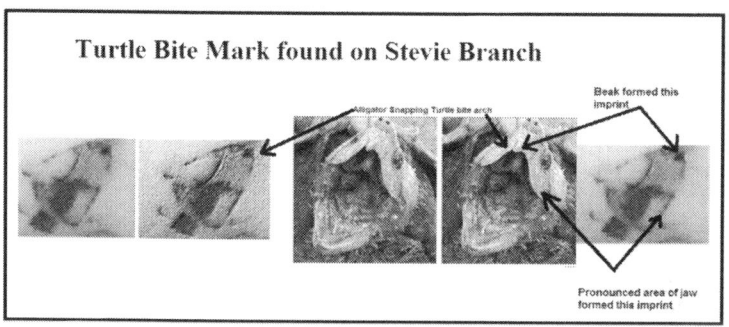

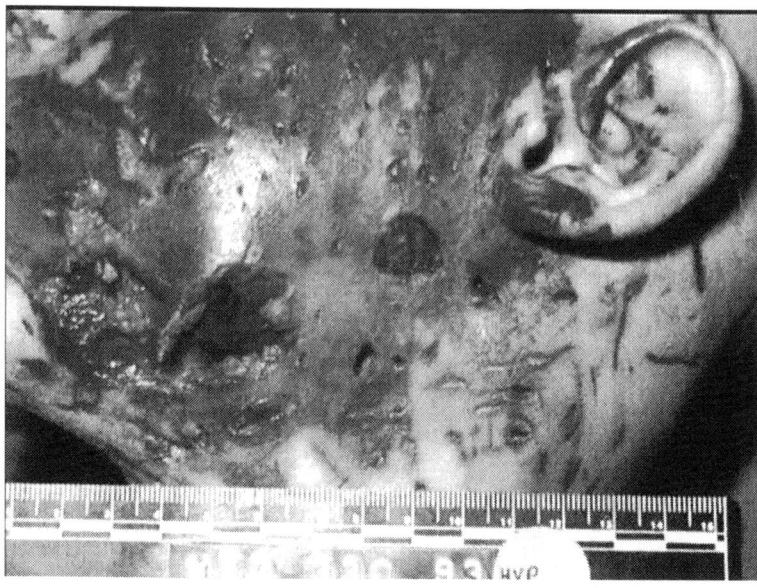

More wounds that may be contributed to turtle bites

An additional explanation (one that seems very plausible) is that the scrapes on the body were caused by the body being dragged across concrete. People that are not familiar with this case may wonder where concrete comes into the equation.

On the property that the boys' bodies were found, was a storm drain manhole. It stuck up out of the ground about 4 feet. It is covered with concrete that was only applied with a trowel and has a very rough surface. When we looked at this drainage manhole, we did notice that the trowel lines were in fact consistent with the scratches on the body.

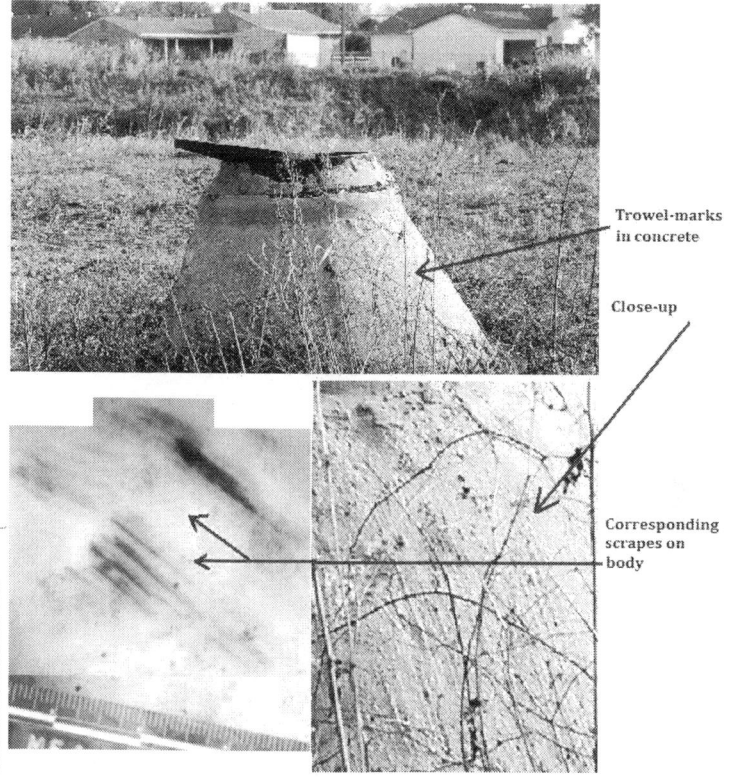

Trowel-marks in concrete

Close-up

Corresponding scrapes on body

We will also note that down inside of the manhole, there were ladder rungs made out of rebar and attached to the wall in a ladder type formation. This is done so a worker can climb in and out of the manhole without any problems.

When we looked at some of the wounds on the body we did discover that these wounds are pretty much 100% consistent with the manhole outer walls and the rebar.

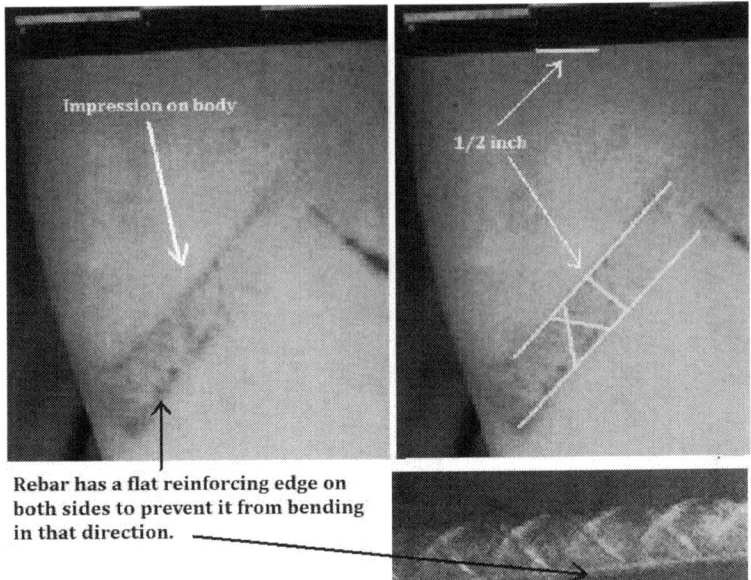

Impression on body

1/2 inch

Rebar has a flat reinforcing edge on
both sides to prevent it from bending
in that direction.

It is a possibility that the boys were in fact killed at the dump site and in an effort to hide the bodies; the killers dropped the 3 boys inside the manhole drain, only to return later and transfer the bodies to the water.

The child pictured above could have had his leg caught behind one of the rebar rungs when being dropped into the drain and that could have caused this impression on his skin.

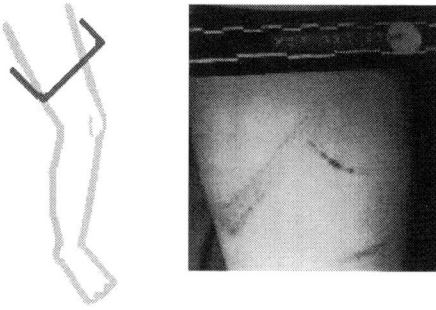

With medical examiner Dr. Frank Peretti on the stand, one of the prosecuting attorneys, Brent Davis, handed him the knife that was discovered in the lake behind Jason's house. Peretti agreed that wounds found on the body of Christopher Byers were "consistent with the serrated portion of that knife." On cross-examination, Peretti stated that the wounds on Byers were equally consistent with another serrated knife, in particular one that belonged to Christopher's step-father, John Mark Byers. The knife wounds to Chris's genital area, Peretti said, were "ante mortem." Chris's scrotum was cut off, and his penis skinned, while he was still alive.

One problem with this theory is that the procedure for this would have been almost impossible to accomplish with the knife that was found in the lake. The removal of the skin on the penis would have been a cut that required great precision and there is no way that could have been done with such an oversized knife blade as the one found in the lake behind Jason Baldwin's house.

One additional theory is that the penis and scrotum were removed, not by any knife, but by the turtles that lived in the water where the children's bodies were dumped. But these two theories have not been proven and the skinning of the penis and removal of the scrotum has been the center of many controversies.

Dr. Peretti also told the jurors that the autopsies revealed that both Steven Branch and Michael Moore received massive blows to their heads, and that Michael's lungs were filled with water, indicating that, "when he was in the water, he was breathing." This could also be caused by water that accumulated in the drainage manhole with the rebar. Experts agree that if Michael was in fact thrown into the manhole first and the other two children thrown on top of him, he would have been submerged in any water that would have been on the bottom of the drain pipe.

Defense attorneys were able to make Dr. Peretti acknowledge on cross-examination that many of the descriptions of the murder that were offered by Jessie Misskelley in his confession were not confirmed by his medical findings.

The prosecution called another key witness in their case, Michael Carson, a sixteen-year-old who had spent some time in jail with Jason Baldwin. He testified that Jason had admitted to him that he "dismembered the kids" and "sucked the blood from the penis and scrotum and put the balls in his mouth." Carson told jurors he decided to come forward with his story, months after his alleged conversation with Jason, because he saw on television how "brokenhearted" the parents of the missing boys were and because "I have got a soft heart. I couldn't take it." Carson's explosive testimony, along with a fiber that was "microscopically similar" to a fiber from a bath robe found inside Jason's home and was found near the bodies of the three victims, represented the entire case that the Prosecution had against Jason Baldwin. (The state's case against Jason was so weak that they had approached his attorneys with an offer to take the life sentence off the table and to ask the judge for a sentence of forty years, with parole being possible after only fifteen years with good behavior, if Jason would just agree to testify against Damien. Jason immediately rejected their offer. He never even considered it as an option.)

Besides the lake knife, there was also a second knife that we briefly mentioned above that belonged to John Mark Byers, the adoptive father (step-father) of victim Christopher Byers that caused some concern in the case.
John Byers gave a knife to one of the camera men named Doug Cooper, who was working with documentary film makers Joe Berlinger and Bruce Sinofsky while they were filming the first *Paradise Lost* documentary for HBO. The knife was a

small utility-type knife. According to the statements that were given by Berlinger and Sinofsky, Cooper told them that he had received the knife on December 19, 1993 as a Christmas gift from John Byers.
After the documentary was filmed, the crew returned to New York. Berlinger and Sinofsky said that they discovered what they thought looked to be blood on the knife. HBO executives ordered them to return the knife to the West Memphis Police Department. The knife was not delivered to the West Memphis Police Department until January 8, 1994.

Byers initially claimed the knife had never been used. Blood was found on the knife, and Byers then stated that he had used it only once, and that was only to cut some deer meat. When he was told that the blood matched both his and Christopher's blood type, Byers said he had no idea how that blood might have gotten on the knife. During interrogation, West Memphis police suggested to Byers that he might have left the knife out accidentally, and Byers said that he assumed that was a possibility, but he didn't believe that he had left it out. Byers later stated that he may have cut his own thumb with it while trying to cut some deer meat thin enough for jerky. Further testing on the knife produced inconclusive results, due in part to the rather small amount of blood that was present, and due to the fact that both John Mark Byers and Christopher Byers had the same HLA-DQα genotype.

Note *Many people believe that "the Byers knife" had Christopher Byers' blood on it. This is not necessarily true. The DNA tests conducted did not have the precision to match the blood to a single individual. The tests just narrowed the blood source to a particular segment of the population, which included both John Mark Byers and Chris Byers.*

John Mark Byers agreed to, and subsequently passed, a polygraph test during the filming of "Paradise Lost 2: Revelations" in regards to the murders, but the documentary indicated that Byers was under the influence of several psychoactive prescription medications that could have affected the test results. Byers also volunteered his false teeth when presented with the challenge he had bit the boys bodies during the filming of the show, although at the time of the murders, he had his original teeth, which he later had voluntarily extracted. He later claimed that there was a medical reason for the procedure, saying that a medication that he had been taking caused his gums to pull away from his teeth. But still another time, he claimed that his teeth were knocked out in a fight with someone who was accusing him of being the one that had killed the three boys.

Besides the disputed knife, the only physical evidence that allegedly connected Damien Echols with the crime was "a trace of blue wax" found on the shirt of one of the murdered boys.

What appeared to be blue candle wax was also found on a book (called *Never on a Broomstick*) in Echols' bedroom. A small blue candle was found on a table in Domini Teer's bedroom. (Domini Teer was Echols' girlfriend at the time). Here is a picture of the blue candle that was in Domini's bedroom.

You may ask, "Why is this important"? Because small amounts of blue candle wax were found on the shirt that was worn by Stevie Branch, one of the victims. It was never proven that the waxes matched, but this strange coincidence was mentioned in the prosecution's closing arguments.

The police also found a polyester fiber recovered from a cub scout cap that, according to Lisa Sakevicius of the state crime lab, was "microscopically similar" to fibers found on a shirt in the Damien Echols' home.

The prosecution wrapped up its case with the testimony of two girls who claimed to have over heard Damien confesses to the murders while attending a softball game. Jodee Medford, a junior high school student, said she was watching the game when she heard Echols, at a distance of about twenty-five feet, say *that he killed*

the three little boys and before he turned
himself in, that he was gonna kill two more
and he already had one of 'em picked out."
On cross-examination, Medford admitted
that even though she had told her mother
about the comments that she had heard,
neither she nor her mother bothered to report
the matter to police. Medford's story
generally matched that of her twelve-year-
old friend, Christy Van Vickle, who
attended the girls' softball game with her
that evening in May 1993.

Many believe that Echols unwittingly
contributed to his own conviction by
refusing to downplay his estrangement from
the community. The HBO documentary
Paradise Lost includes a fair amount of
footage from the original trial, including
Echols being cross-examined by the
prosecution, and while he's a fascinating
personality, he rarely comes across as

anything other than a polite, cooperative kid who's answering every question as honestly as he can.

The Prosecutor knew that they needed to show the jury the connection between Damien Echols and the occult. First, attorney for the State Brent Davis, asked Echols whether he was familiar with a man by the name of Aleister Crowley. He introduced a sheet of paper on which Echols had practiced writing in some sort of cipher, using Crowley's name alongside that of his own name as well as the names of family and friends. The implication is that Echols is much more of a Crowley fan than he had let on, although it's hard to say exactly what conclusion a sensible jury is meant to draw from such a revelation, even if they should decide to accept it.

Here are some of the transcripts from Damien's actual testimony when he was asked about Aleister Crowley during his trial.

Q. After that, you studied and looked into the satanic side of the occult, correct?

A. Um-hum.

Q. And you were familiar with it, right?

A. I'm familiar with about every aspect of it.

Q. You're familiar with a fellow named Aleister Crowley?

A. I know who he is.

Q. He is a guy who kindly professes -- he is a noted author in the field of satanic worship, right?

A. I know who he is, but I have never saw any of his books personally.

Q. Not much of a follower of his?

A. I would have read them if I had saw them.

Q. But Aleister Crowley is a guy that based on his writings believes in human sacrifice, doesn't he?

A. He also believed he was God so --

Q. He also had writings that indicated that children were the best type of human sacrifice, right?

A. Yes, sir.

Q. But Aleister Crowley doesn't have any particular significance to you?

A. I know who he is. I have read a little bit about him, but I have never read anything by him.

Q. Let me show you a copy of some documents. Do you recognize that?

A. Yes.

Q. What is that?

A. It was this paper I had on different alphabets or like translations where you could write things that nobody could read. This was one of the forms.

Q. Where did you have that at? When did you do that?

A. Sometime before I was arrested I guess.

Q. Are you sure you have not done those since you were arrested while you've been staying in the jail?

A. I don't know. I might have.

Q. What kind of -- is that alphabet up there -- is that some sort of Wiccan alphabet?

A. I don't remember in particular what this one is.

Q. Whose names are written on that document?

A. Mine, Jason's, my son's, one that says Aleister Crowley --

Q. Who?

A. Aleister Crowley.

Q. This is a document that you have written while you have been waiting in jail for trial, right?

A. If you say so.

Q. Well, you wrote it. That's your writing, correct?

A. Um-hum.

Q. Do you recall when you wrote it?

A. Not really. There's five more that I don't know what is there.

Q. What you were doing is writing out various names in different type alphabets, correct?

A. From the way it looks here, I was practicing trying to memorize them.

Q. One of the names that you picked out to write about was this fellow named Aleister Crowley?

A. Um-hum.

Q. Is that just a total coincidence? You just pulled his name out of the air?

A. It is the same book that I had with the different alphabets and it also had stuff about him.

Q. Did you have the book out there at the time you were doing this?

A. This is from what I remembered myself. I was practicing, trying to memorize, getting it all in my head.

Q. So you were going over it working on it

in your head and at that point in time you write all this down from memory?

A. Um-hum.

Q. Had you studied Aleister's book pretty carefully?

A. Never any book by him in particular. I have never saw any of his.

The prosecution team wanted to paint Damien as a Satan worshiper. The prosecutors did in fact make one connection with this testimony. It helped in showing the jury that Damien did in fact have at the very least, an interest in the occult. The fact that Damien listed the name of his best friend and his own son's right alongside of that of Aleister Crowley, made the jurors believe that Aleister Crowley may have played more of an important role in Damien's life than he was leading them to believe.

Damien answered all the questions calmly and plainly, as if he were just a witness and not actually one of the defendants in his own murder trial. One could argue that Berlinger and Sinofsky, whose film pretty clearly tried to portray the West Memphis Three as wrongly convicted, were selective about what they chose to include and omit, deliberately making Echols look as innocent as possible. Damien also blew kisses at the victim's families, though that was purposely not in the documentary. On the stand, however, he never comes across as arrogant or belligerent or even especially "creepy".

The Defense's case

After opening its case with testimony from Pam Echols, who told jurors that her son (Damien) had spent the night of the murders at home with her and that he had phone conversations with two girlfriends, (This was proven to be false according to the statements of the two girls); the defense then called Damien to the stand. Val Price asked Damien about his family history and his interests, which Damien said included skateboarding, movies, talking on the phone, and reading. He then asked Damien about his focus on the Wicca religion, which Damien explained was "basically a close involvement with nature." "I'm not a Satanist," Damien insisted. "I don't believe in human sacrifices or anything like that." Price then asked Damien to read excerpts from his personal journal, which included favorite quotes such as "Life is but a walking shadow. It is a tale told by an idiot, full of sound and fury, signifying nothing," from Shakespeare's "A Midsummer Night's Dream." He was also asked why he kept a dog skull in his bedroom, Damien replied, "I just thought it was kind of cool." Asked why he had the word "evil" tattooed across his knuckles, Damien had a similar answer: "I just kinda thought it was cool, so I did that." When he was asked about why he always wore black, Damien responded, "I was told that I look good in black. And I'm real self-conscious, uh, the way I dress." The defense sought to present Damien as a teenager who might be different from most in West Memphis, but not as someone anyone should fear. Echols denied having anything to do with the deaths of the three boys. He testified, "I'd never even heard of them before 'til I saw it on the news." Asked how he felt about being charged with the murders, he said, "Sometimes angry, sometimes sad, sometimes scared."

The defense then focused on the police investigation. Gary Gitchell admitted that although West Memphis owned a video camera and audio recorders, they had not bothered to tape any of their interviews with

Damien. Gitchell also admitted that blood samples left on the wall of a Bojangles restaurant on the evening of the murder were "as the term is, lost."

John Mark Byers was called to testify about the knife he had given an HBO film crew member. Byers testified that the blood found on the knife was his, coming from a cut, despite the fact that he had repeatedly told authorities he had "no idea" how human blood ended up on his knife.

The defense's plan to call Christopher Morgan, a teenager who once confessed (and later recanted) to California police that *he* might have "blacked out" and killed the three boys in West Memphis, was thwarted when his attorney announced in a hearing before Judge Burnett (from which the press was excluded) that his client, if forced to testify, would invoke his Fifth Amendment rights against self-incrimination.

Prosecutors argued that Morgan's pleading the Fifth, which Morgan's attorney insisted related to a pending federal drug charge against his client that might be vaguely related to the murders, would mislead the jury, who would quite naturally conclude that Morgan was hiding his involvement in the actual murders of the three boys. Burnett ruled that he would not force Morgan to testify and said that anyone who mentioned his ruling to the press "or anyone else...will be held in contempt, and I mean it."

The defense called their final witness, Robert Hicks, a police training officer with expertise about satanic crime. Hicks testified that he knew of no connection between sexual mutilation and the occult. He also told jurors that "we do have empirical evidence" that listening to Metallica music does not "lead people to commit crimes." He described the phrase "trappings of the occult," used by the prosecution's "expert" Dale Griffis, as "absolutely meaningless in considering any kind of violent crime."

The defense rested. Jason Baldwin never testified, his attorney hoping that his client's low profile and the very little evidence against him would save his client. "We wanted to just disappear on the radar screen and let Damien be the whole focus," Paul Ford would later say. "We thought that if we didn't stir the pot, and they didn't stir the pot, what were they going to convict him on?"

On March 17, 1994, the jury listened to closing arguments. John Fogleman argued that while most people might not believe "this satanic stuff," what "matters is what these defendants believe." Religion, he said, "is a motivating force. It gives people who want to do evil, want to commit murders, a reason to do what they're doing." Fogleman also told the jurors that when "you see inside Damien, and you look inside there, there's not a soul there." Val Price, the lead defense attorney for Damien Echols, reminded jurors that the law required them to find his client guilty beyond a reasonable doubt--and, after listening to the evidence, they should have plenty of doubts. He pointed to the blood found on the knife owned by John Mark Byers, the bloody man who entered a local Bojangles restaurant about the time of the murders, and the almost non- existent physical evidence connecting Damien with the murders. He argued that having "weird things in your room...doesn't mean you're guilty of murder." Paul Ford delivered the closing argument for Jason Baldwin, arguing that the prosecution hoped jurors would find his client "guilty by association." "Take the blindfolds off," he told jurors, and look at this case "the way it really is--and send

Jason Baldwin home." The final argument belonged to prosecutor Brent Davis. Summing up, Davis said, "We have presented a circumstantial case with circumstantial evidence, and it's good enough for conviction." He told jurors "you can feel good" about convicting both of these defendants.

The Verdict and Sentence

The following afternoon jurors returned to the courtroom with their verdicts. Both defendants were guilty of capital murder in the deaths of all three boys. Family members of the murdered boys cheered and hugged. Jason cried, while Damien showed little emotion. Terry Hobbs, Stevie Branch's step-father, told reporters he hoped that both defendants would be executed: "Those guys took a life, let them lose a life." He also said that he only wished he could have "ten minutes alone" with Baldwin and Echols "to do to them what they did to the boys."

In a second phase of the trial to determine sentencing, the jury listened to evidence relating to aggravating and mitigating circumstances for each of the two defendants. After listening to several hours of testimony, much of it concerning Damien's mental state and statements he had made to a therapist, the jury returned to the jury room and began scribbling out "pros" and "cons" for Jason and for Damien. Jason earned several "pros": "stuck to story," "exhibited remorse," and "in school." He got "cons" for being "Damien's best friend," his "jailhouse confession," "low self-esteem," and "frequented crime scene."

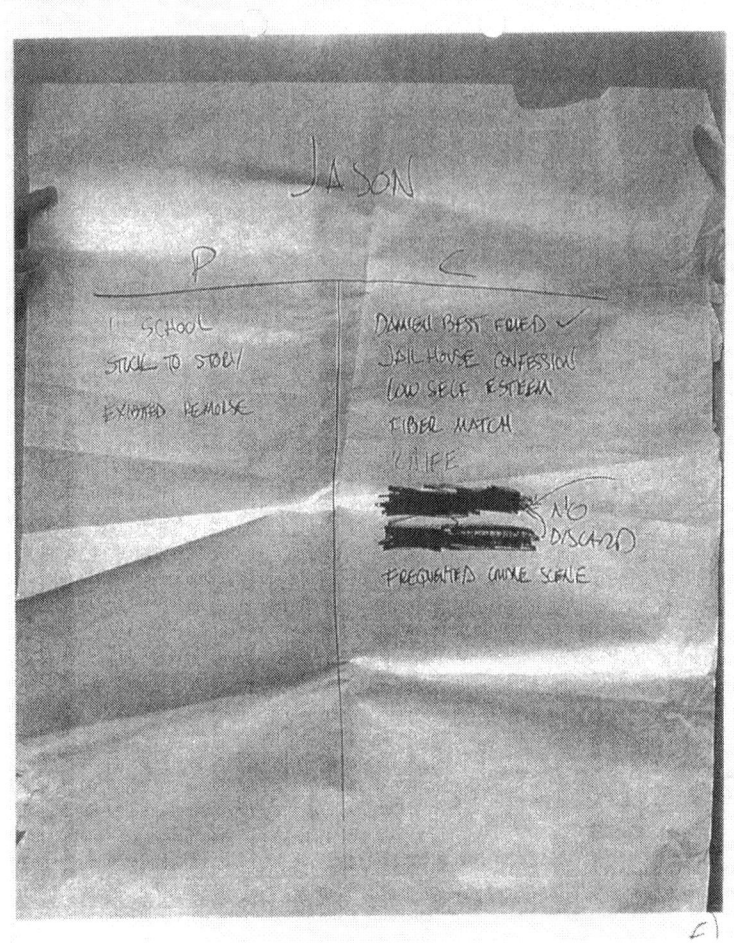

Damien got "pros" only for being "intelligent" and "manic depressive," for having a "loyal family," and for sticking to his story. His long list of negatives, however, included "Satanic follower," "manipulative," "dishonest," "weird,"

"something to gain," "blew kisses to parents," "inappropriate thought patterns," and "eat father alive."

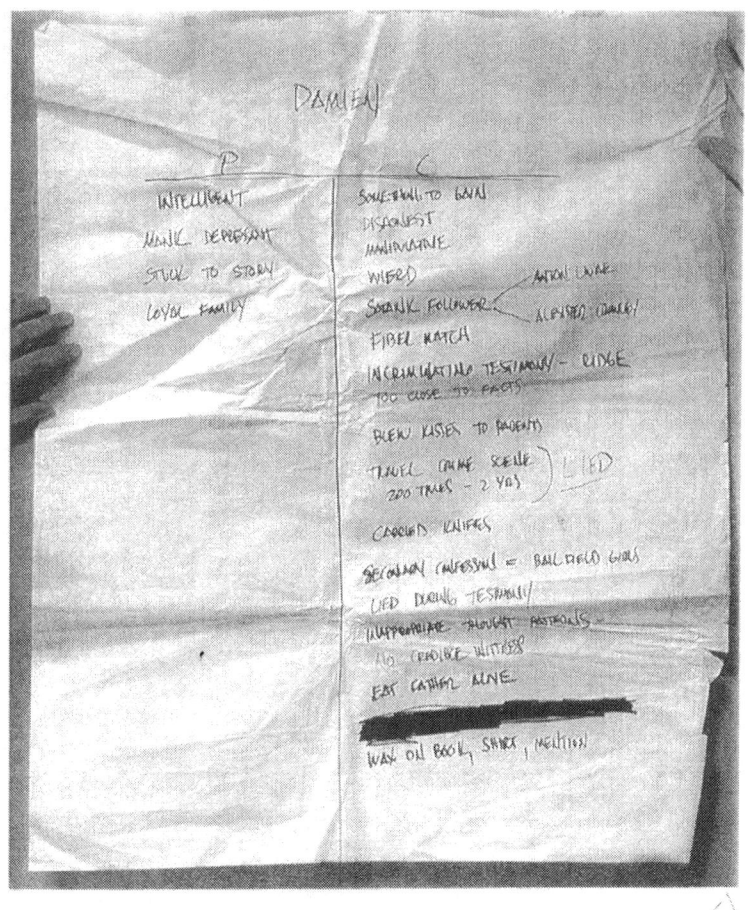

The jurors decided to sentence Jason, who was just 16 at the time of the murders, to life in prison without the possibility of parole. But as for Damien, the jurors decided that he should be sentenced to death by lethal injection. After Judge Burnett sentenced Damien Echols to die on May 5, 1994, exactly a year to the day after Michael Moore, Steven Branch and Christopher Byers were killed; both defendants were led out of the Jonesboro courtroom. Jason Baldwin was transported to the penitentiary at Pine Bluff, while Damien Echols began life on death row in the state's maximum security prison near Varner, Arkansas.

CHAPTER EIGHT

THE HUNT CONTINUES

As Damien Echols, Jason Baldwin and Jessie Misskelley sat in the Arkansas State prison system, a movement began to happen all over the country to free the three men convicted of murdering three children in West Memphis. They even gained the support of numerous celebrities, including actors, actresses and stars in both country and rock music.

Many people believe that the support was solely based on the notion that the three were convicted on the basis of the music that they listened to rather than the evidence of the case. Some called the trial a witch hunt and that the three were labeled Satan worshipers because they listened to music by Metallica, a heavy metal rock band famous at the time of the murders. Others feel that the police focused their entire energy on building a case against the three rather than pursuing the real facts of the case.

But whatever the reason for the following, they brought attention to the case and kept the story alive for many years after the trial ended.

Arkansas Supreme Court ruling

On November 4, 2010, the Arkansas Supreme Court ordered a lower judge to consider whether newly analyzed DNA evidence might exonerate the three. The justices also said a lower court must examine claims of misconduct by the jurors who sentenced Damien Echols to death and Jessie Misskelley and Jason Baldwin to life in prison.

HERE IS THE NEWS RELEASE ISSUED REGARDING THE MOTION

(Little Rock, AR, May 2, 2011) — In his motion for a new trial, Damien Echols today submitted a "Brief on The Admissibility of Evidence of Juror Misconduct," in which he asks presiding Judge David Laser to admit evidence of juror misconduct at his first trial in this proceeding. He also asks the judge to conduct oral arguments and allow testimony at the hearing scheduled to begin December 5, 2011.

The filing goes into detail about how police obtained Misskelley's so-called confession during his interrogation, how the prosecution introduced it via news reports prior to the trials, and how the jury came to consider the inadmissible "confession" during its deliberations.

The filing includes shocking evidence that the jury foreman at the Echols/Baldwin trial, Kent Arnold, allegedly lied to the court during jury selection so that he would be sure to be selected and that he allegedly introduced Misskelley's false confession into jury deliberations although it was constitutionally barred from consideration because Misskelley refused to testify.

Lloyd Warford, a prominent Arkansas attorney, former prosecutor, and state official, submitted a sworn affidavit detailing a dozen improper conversations that Kent Arnold held with him while the original trial was in progress, clearly violating the law and the rights of Echols and Baldwin to a fair and impartial trial. In those conversations, juror Arnold indicates that he had prejudged Echols's guilt and was trying to convince other jurors to convict them based upon news reports of the false confession of Misskelley, portions of which had even been published in newspapers before the trial.

During one conversation, Arnold informed attorney Warford that the prosecution had presented a weak case and that the

prosecution had better present something
powerful the next day (the end of the
prosecution's case) or it would be up to him
to secure a conviction.

According to the legal briefs, "... Echols
contended in his 2008 motion, and asserts
again here, that the 1994 judgments were
fundamentally flawed and unreliable, and
thus are not entitled to a presumption of
validity. Rather than being convicted on
"evidence developed [on] the witness stand
in a public courtroom where there is full
judicial protection of the defendant's right of
confrontation, of cross-examination, and of
counsel," Turner v. Louisiana, 379 U.S. 466,
472-73 (1965), Echols was found guilty
principally based on what biased jurors had
heard and read outside the courtroom.
Echols's jury convicted him based on
information both unadmitted and
inadmissible at trial: media reports
concerning a demonstrably false statement

of codefendant Jessie Misskelley implicating Echols and Baldwin in the charged crimes. Mr. Echols contends that, to the contrary, the prior convictions must be afforded no weight whatsoever in the court's calculus of the likelihood of acquittal because, tainted by misconduct of the most egregious and blatant sort, their probative value on that crucial issue is nil. Indeed, the evidence of misconduct now on file before this court makes clear that Mr. Echols and Mr. Baldwin were convicted in 1994 only because the jury foreman relied on information that was not only inadmissible, but demonstrably false, to convince his fellow jurors to vote for guilt."

In a separate filing, attorneys for Baldwin, state, "Baldwin has tendered ample evidence of misconduct by his original jury as part of his Petition/Motion for New Trial, including the record of the jury selection, affidavits, juror notes, and other evidence demonstrating that the original verdict was tainted by misconduct."

Lorri Davis, wife of Damien Echols and co-founder of "Arkansas Take Action", said, "We ask the court to consider the seriousness of the juror misconduct in Jason and Damien's trial, as well as the evidence that Jessie Misskelley's confession was just plain false."

In early December 2010, Circuit Court Judge David Laser was selected to replace David Burnett, who had been elected to the Arkansas State Senate, to preside in the evidentiary hearings following the successful appeal.

Plea deal and release

After weeks of negotiations, on August 19, 2011, Echols, Baldwin and Misskelley were released from prison as part of an Alford plea deal, a legal mechanism in which "guilty" pleas are entered but innocence is nevertheless maintained. An Alford plea concedes that prosecutors have sufficient evidence to secure a conviction but reserves the right to assert innocence. Stephen Braga, an attorney with Ropes & Gray who took up Echols's defense beginning in 2009, negotiated the plea agreement with prosecutors. Under the deal, Judge David Laser vacated the previous convictions, including the capital murder convictions for Echols and Baldwin, and ordered a new trial. Each man then entered an Alford plea to lesser charges of first- and second-degree murder while verbally stating their innocence. Judge Laser then sentenced them to time served, a total of 18 years and 78 days, and they were given a suspended imposition of sentence for 10 years. If they re-offend in that time period they can be sent back to prison for 21 years.

The Alford plea deal meant that the hearing ordered by the Arkansas Supreme Court in November 2010, scheduled for December

2011 before Judge Laser, became unnecessary. Factors cited by prosecutor Scott Ellington for agreeing to the plea deal included that two of the victims' families have joined forces with the defense, the mother of a witness who testified about Echols's confession has questioned her daughter's truthfulness, and the State Crime Lab employee who collected fiber evidence at the Echols and Baldwin homes after their arrests has died. In addition to the plea deal, they cannot pursue civil action against the state for wrongful imprisonment.

Many of their supporters as well as opponents who still believe them guilty resented the unusual plea deal. Supporters are pushing Arkansas Governor Mike Beebe to pardon Echols, Baldwin and Misskelley based on evidence of their innocence. Beebe stated that he plans to deny any requests until solid evidence is found showing someone else committed the murders. Prosecutor Scott Ellington said the

Arkansas state crime laboratory would run
searches on any DNA evidence produced in
private laboratory tests in the defense's
investigation. Ellington said that although he
still considered the men guilty, the three
would likely be acquitted if a new trial were
held given the powerful legal counsel
representing them now, the loss of evidence
over time, and the change of heart among
some of the witnesses.

ADDITIONAL SUSPECTS

Over the years the supporters of the West Memphis Three have come to numerous conclusions on the identities of the real killer or killers.

We will look at the prime suspects that have been named in this case by the support groups and look at the facts and the myths concerning each one. Our purpose is not to point to any one person and claim that they are the real killer or killers. We want to present all of the facts as we see them to you, the reader, and let you come to your own decision.

Terry Hobbs, Chris Morgan, Brian Holland, LG Hollingsworth, and David Jacoby

At a hearing held in March 2013 regarding evidence in the West Memphis Three murders, the names of several new possible suspects were released by attorneys for

Pamela Hicks the mother of Steven Branch. Several documents were handed out naming new possible suspects in the 1993 murders of three 8-year-old boys.

One of those named is Terry Hobbs, her ex-husband and the step-father of Stevie. Also on the list are the names David Jacoby, LG Hollingsworth and Buddy Lucas.

Bennie Guy, who once lived with Lucas, stated that Lucas had confessed to him about committing the murders. Guy says Lucas confessed to the killings on two separate instances.

According to Guy's affidavit, Hollingsworth said the group had spotted the three boys after smoking weed and drinking whiskey. Hobbs demanded they catch the boys. But after one of the boys kicked him, Hobbs became enraged and started to beat the child. Then the others started to severely beat the other two boys. According to the Affidavit, Hobbs forced Hollingsworth and Lucas to strip the boy's pants off, and then Hobbs cut the groin of one child and then tossed the boys bodies in a ditch. Guy says Hollingsworth showed no remorse. But there is no mention of the shoe laces in the story. Maybe Hobbs went back later in the day and tied the boys and dumped the bodies in the water? Jacoby says, "there was a window Mr. Hobbs wasn't with me and I never spoke out on that because I'm thinking if West Memphis Three was railroaded how hard would it be to railroad him if I was to say he was missing for a couple of hours."

Lucas, who is described as being mentally 'slow,' was reportedly sent away from the area for several years immediately after the incident. Bennie Guy said that the West Memphis Police never returned his call regarding this information he had provided.

When our investigators spoke to the West Memphis Police regarding why this call was not returned, they were told that the information that was provided by the caller did not coincide with the evidence at the crime scene.

The caller stated that Hobbs stabbed the boys repeatedly and that each boy was punched in the face multiple times prior to being killed. The medical examiner did not find wounds that matched the beating or stabbing that the caller claimed happened to the boys. They went on to say that if the boys had been beaten as bad as the caller said, that there would have been numerous signs of facial injuries and broken or fractured bones in the face that would have been found during the autopsy. They also noted that the caller never mentioned that the boys had been tied up. This would have been information that would have prompted a closer look into the information that this person was providing.

The West Memphis Police and the Arkansas State police have received numerous phone tips over the years claiming that they had solid information to prove that Terry Hobbs and the other three teenagers killed the boys. But the information that the callers provide do not match the facts of the investigation.

One thing we do know is that there was blood found between the storm drain and the location where the bodies were found. We also know that there were scrape wounds on the body that match the concrete patterns on the side of the manhole. Not to mention the wound patterns found on the leg that matches rebar that is used in the manhole as ladder steps.

When we look at this information and the statements that were made, we can conclude the following as the events of the crime.

NOTE

This is just a theory of what could have happened and I am not putting this forth as solid proof of the crime.

The group spotted the three boys watching them smoking weed and drinking whiskey, just as Hollingsworth said. Terry Hobbs demanded they catch the boys. During the struggle, one of the boys kicked Hobbs; he became enraged and started to beat the child. Then the others started to severely beat the other two boys. Maybe it was not so severe as to break bones or cause fractures. Now it was said that Hobbs forced Hollingsworth and Lucas to strip the boy's pants off, and then Hobbs cut the groin of one child and then tossed the boys bodies in a ditch. We don't necessarily believe the part where the groin was cut. The cutting of the groin area is usually associated with a sexual undertone of a crime. And we don't feel that this crime was sexually motivated at all. However, if the first boy kicked Hobbs in his testicles, then it may be feasible that he did wound the child in the groin area as a retaliation move. The bodies could have been moved from the spot of the beatings and dropped inside the manhole which would explain the blood found between the woods and the location of the manhole.

As the bodies are dropped in to the manhole they are dragged across the outer edge of the manhole causing the scratches on the bodies that match the trowel marks on the side of the manhole.

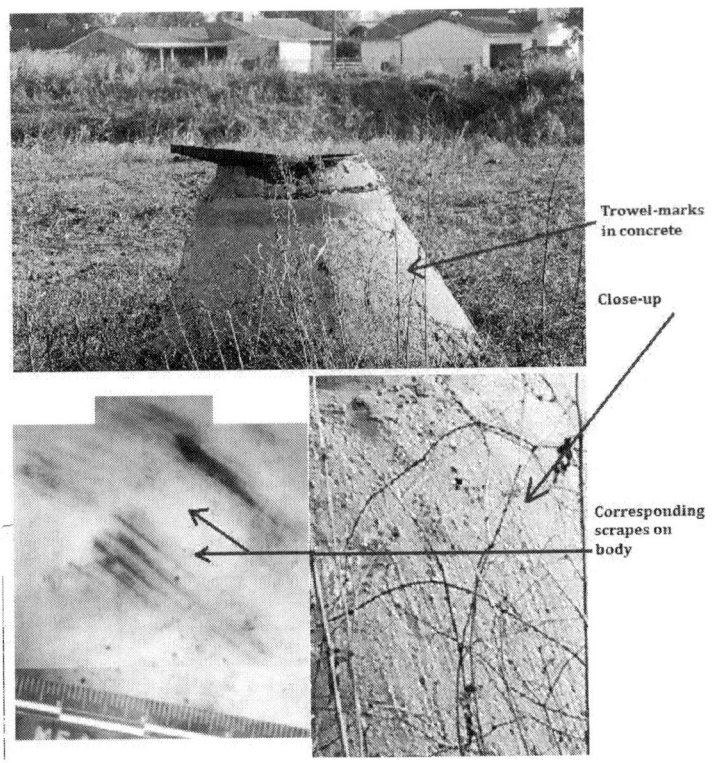

Trowel-marks in concrete

Close-up

Corresponding scrapes on body

And when they are dropped in the leg of one of the children could have gotten lodged behind the ladder rung that is made from rebar, causing the wound pattern on the child's leg that matches the pattern of rebar.

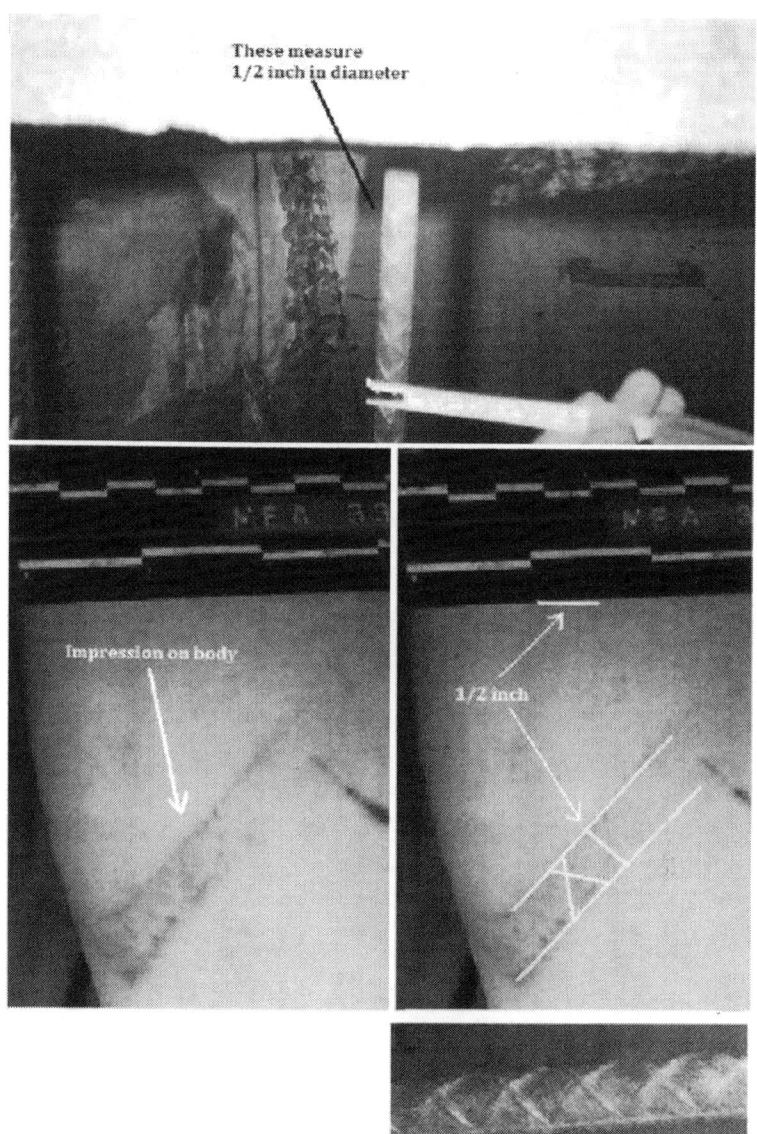

These measure
1/2 inch in diameter

Impression on body

1/2 inch

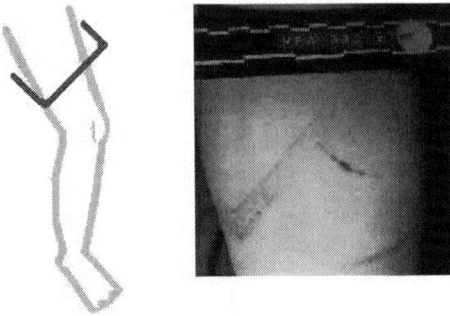

When we look at the fact that the part where the boys were tied up was left out of the confession by Hollingsworth that also could easily be explained. Terry Hobbs could have returned later in the evening with someone besides Hollingsworth and removed the boys from the manhole. They could have then tied up the bodies and placed them into the water. Hollingsworth never mentioned this because he may not have been involved in this part of the crime. This could have been done in the two hour time frame that David Jacoby says that Terry was not accounted for.

In May 2013, Terry Hobbs spoke with Channel 3 News and spoke in depth about the fact that he was being implicated in the murders.

Here are the transcripts from that interview.

The following article and news cast was published in May (2013) by WREG Channel 3 News.

(Memphis) It's a murder mystery that's captivated America for the last twenty years: the West Memphis Three

All these years later, the country is still divided on who murdered those three little boys in Arkansas in 1993.

Many have theories, including one where Terry Hobbs, the step-father of one of the boys, is the killer. Hobbs hasn't done a TV interview in years, but agreed to sit down with WREG's Sabrina Hall to answer some questions.

Terry Hobbs says he is a church member, a father, and working man and in no way a killer.

"Everyone has a story and this just happens to be mine," said Hobbs.

What a story it is.

It's one that's sparked documentaries, a handful of books, even a movie that is about to be released.

"With Hollywood actors," said Hobbs.

"And who is playing your wife?" asked Hall.

"Reese Witherspoon," laughed Hobbs. *"I am happy about that."*

Hobbs can find humor in a story that's brought him so much pain over the last twenty years, *"There is not a day that goes by, seriously, that you don't think about it."*

On May 6, 1993, three boys are found hog-tied and murdered in a ditch in West

Memphis, Arkansas. One of the 8-year-olds is Hobbs' stepson, Stevie Branch.

"He would have been a heart breaker if he grew up. Blonde hair, blue eyes," said Hobbs.

West Memphis police believe the killers to be three teenagers in a satanic cult: Damien Echols, Jason Baldwin and Jessie Misskelley. Misskelley even confessed to the crime, a confession Hobbs says he heard because he sat through every day of their trials.

"They are guilty," said Hobbs. Hobbs says he believes that with all his heart, yet many have a different theory on who killed those boys.

"Terry Wayne Hobbs," said Mark Byers, a father of one of the victims, in a previous interview. *"I don't know how much clearer I have to make it."*

That theory is the premise of the latest documentary "West of Memphis".

"In the middle of a knot that had been tightened, there was hair jammed in the middle of that knot," said a forensic expert in the film.

Forensic experts say DNA evidence ties Hobbs to the crime scene and that neighbors saw him with the boys that night. Hobbs says the hair found could be his, *"all those little boys played at our home."* But says the rest of the accusations in the documentary are false.

"So you didn`t even see them that day at all?" asked Hall.

"No," said Hobbs.

"So why do people say they saw you outside and you were calling them home?" asked Hall.

"Because people can," said Hobbs.
*"People can say whatever they want to say.
It doesn't make it true."*

Hobbs says when he got home from work on
May 5, 1993, the boys were already out
riding their bikes, he never them saw them
again. Yet, theories keep coming that point
to Hobbs as the man behind the murders.

*"This is not a theory of who did this, this is
evidence,"* said an attorney.

Just this March, lawyers for Hobbs' ex-wife,
Pam Hicks, and the father of another victim,
Mark Byers, paint a more detailed picture:
that Hobbs killed the boys with three other
men after a day of drinking and smoking
pot. Hobbs says the entire story is a
complete fabrication.

*"There should be a time when you draw the
line and you say 'you don't cross this line'
and it's been crossed,"* said Hobbs.

Hobbs says he is a victim in the story and has even tried to file lawsuits against those who've said otherwise but says, because he's seen as a public figure, lawyers tell him that he doesn't have a case. In the end, he says he lives with it, *"At some point you've got say 'I got to keep on going. This thing will beat you down if you let it and I chose not to let it control my life."*

Hobbs says his ex-wife knows he is innocent, *"She knows better."*

But says Hicks, as well Byers, are wrapped-up in a story that's turned into an industry, *"To me, they've all tried to capitalize and they have turned our tragedy into a money making business."*

He says that business, and Hollywood hype, has set the real killers free, *"Jason Baldwin, Damien Echols and Jessie Misskelley. I believe that with everything inside of me."*

Hobbs says he hopes the three eventually tell the truth one day and apologize, but until then Hobbs says he has to live with the story that many people believe.

"Do you wish you had a different story?" asked Hall.

"Well sure," said Hobbs. *"I am as human as anybody else and I don't like to be portrayed as a bad person because I am not."*

Hobbs says he has considered contacting the makers of the Devil's Knot, the movie coming out this year, to find out if they are portraying him as a bad guy. Instead, he's decided to be surprised like the rest of us.

When we look at this interview one thing stands out: Hobbs says that he did not see the boys on the day of the murders. BUT, a neighbor gave a statement to the West Memphis Police that she saw the boys riding their bikes through her yard and that Terry was yelling for them. She even stated that she saw all three boys in the company of Terry as she and her family drove out of their driveway to go to church that day. To some, this may seem trivial and not important. But we have to ask ourselves this: Why would Terry Hobbs deny seeing the boys on that day if he really did see them? He could have easily said that he called the boys to him as the witness stated and he could have said that the boys rode off to play after he spoke to them.

We know that there are fanatics out there now that will doctor images to prove a fact in this case. During the research process for this book, we came across hundreds of West Memphis Three supporters that are so zealous and biased about this case that they are spewing lies all over the internet to try and convince the world that the three charged and convicted are innocent. But the eye witness who saw Terry Hobbs that day with the boys had no motive to lie about what she saw. At the time, this was a fresh case and the world was not full of the misconceptions and biased opinions that are present today regarding this case.

It is known that a suspect will do whatever he can to disassociate himself with the victim of a murder if they are questioned. They believe that it is better to say that they never saw the victim on the day of the murder than to admit that they had a brief encounter. This is called disassociation of guilt. Once the police can prove that the victim and the suspect had interactions on the day of the crime, it only strengthens the suspicions against the suspect.

When we spoke to the West Memphis police as to why Terry was not looked at closer at the time of the initial investigation, we were told that the case against Damien Echols was a more solid case to pursue due to the fact that they knew that Damien was lying in regards to his whereabouts on the day of the murders. The fact that Damien's alibis all fell through and that his own mother's statements contradicted the time line that Damien had provided to the police, made him a viable suspect at the time.

The next thing that we need to look at is the DNA and physical evidence found at the scene that some say without a doubt tie Terry Hobbs to the murders. During the investigation a human hair that was believed to belong to Terry Hobbs was discovered on a shoe lace used to bind Michael Moore.

The West Memphis Three supporters use this information to seal the case against Terry Hobbs. But with every tabloid rumor, most of the information is left out of the story.

We do know that a hair fiber was discovered on the shoe lace used to tie Michael Moore. And if we just look at that information in and of itself, we could say that without a doubt Terry is guilty or at the very least was present at the crime scene during the murders or during the tying of the bodies.

When we questioned about the hair fiber that was found, we were told that the presence of the hair alone does not place a person at a crime scene if they live in the same home. This is called "secondary transfer". In other words, a mother could hug her child and leave hair fibers on the child's clothing. Or a child could pick up hair fibers just by walking through their own home.

We pointed out that the fiber was actually found on Michael Moore's bindings and not Stevie's. We asked if that fact would eliminate the secondary transfer theory. We were told "no". There are a couple of reasons for this. One is the fact that Michael did in fact visit Stevie's home often and could have picked up the hair at the time of a visit. But the investigator had doubts on that theory. As it turns out, the information that has been widely spread on the hair fiber evidence has been twisted so much that the truth is not even part of the story anymore.

The investigator we had been speaking to referred us to the actual trial testimony of Lisa Sakevicius, a criminalist with the State Crime Laboratory. According to Lisa Sakevicius in her courtroom testimony, Stevie Branch was tied with two different shoe laces.

20 Q. On Exhibit 81 — if you would refer to that exhibit.
21 A. That is from Steve Branch.
22 Q. What were your findings as to the knots on Exhibit 81?
23 A. Examination of the ligatures revealed a black shoestring on
24 the right side tied in three half hitches with an extra loop
25 around the leg to a single half hitch with a figure eight around
1509

1 the right wrist. The left side consisted of a white shoestring

2 tied in three half hitches around the wrist to three half
3 hitches around the leg.
4 Q. So on the left side on the wrist you had three half
5 hitches?
6 A. Correct.
7 Q. And on the ankle you had three half hitches?
8 A. Correct.
9 Q. On the right side on the leg you had three half hitches
10 with what?
11 A. An extra loop around the right leg.
12 Q. On the wrist you had?
13 A. A figure eight.
14 Q. With one half hitch. Is that right?
15 A. Yes, sir.

The hair that was connected to Terry was located on a shoe lace used to bind Michael Moore, but as seen by the above testimony, Stevie was tied up with two different laces.

This means that the lace used to bind Michael could have been Stevie's, which would support the secondary transfer theory.

There has been an ongoing joke with the West Memphis police that there were actually three different agencies investigating this case. The West Memphis Police, Arkansas State police and the West Memphis Three supporters.

The supporters of the West Memphis Three use the partial information as grounds to point to the guilt of Terry Hobbs. But all that this really shows is that the DNA test only proves that Terry Hobbs had been in the same home as Stevie. It doesn't actually connect him to the crime. Even if it were Michael's shoe lace, it would still be the same, since the boys were best friends, and often played in each other's houses. All that can be really said for certain about the hair is that it is secondary transfer, and was likely brought to the scene by the victims themselves.

Also found near the crime scene was a second strand of hair found on a tree stump. The defense and supporters of the West Memphis Three have tried to claim that the hair belonged to Terry Hobbs' friend, David Jacoby. When the hair was tested, it was determined to match over 7% of the population. The second strand of hair would not be found until two weeks after the bodies had been discovered. This meant that the hair could have come from anywhere, and belonged to dozens of people, including investigators, searchers, and family and friends of the victims, who had been to the scene since the crime had occurred.

This does not rule out the possibility that Terry Hobbs and his teenage friends killed the boys. It just shows the facts surrounding the hair fibers found at the crime scene. One thing that we can determine from the testimony of Lisa Sakevicius is that there were at least two killers. We can determine this because of the different ways of tying knots that were used to bind the bodies of the victims. The investigators used the facts that the tying pattern was different from each location which supports their theory of multiple killers.

Some other information that has been released in this case is a statement that Pam Hobbs' sister, Jo Lynn, had witnessed Terry washing all the bedding, clothing and curtains in Stevie's room on the night of the murders.

On June 19, 2007 Jo Lynn made the following statement:

Jo Lynn: *I arrived after they found the boys. The family was all at Pam and Terry's home. My dad was there and my mother uh my sisers, my brother they had all arrived. I may have been the fourth or fith person to arrive. By that time they had it on the news showing that they had found the bicycles the boys and it was uh a reality to us at that time.*

The main thing that I want to point out in her June 2007 statement is that she states that she arrived AFTER they had found the boys.

But in 2009 she has a totally new story to tell. Here is her statement in 2009.

Jo Lynn's deposition: May 20, 2009 14. *Other new evidence was provided by me. I was at Pam and Terry's house on May 6, 1993. I personally saw Terry wash clothes, bed linens and curtains at an odd hour. It was very strange to me that he would do all of that laundry at such a horrible time. It was also strange that he was not just washing the dirty laundry, but was also taking clothes out of the dresser drawers and washing those, too.*

It was my opinion that there was no other reason or pressing need that I am aware of for Terry to do that laundry at that time other than to hide evidence of the crimes.

Some experts feel that Jo Lynn changed her story (or added this detail) during the height of the publicity of this case. Pam even came forward to contradict the statement made by Jo Lynn.

This is Pam's response to Jo Lynn's statement concerning the laundry.

Terry made his sister move out before Stevie was murdered probably a month before. She was not questioned until last year when Terry and I were questioned and statements were taken by audio and video which was not done in 93. No Jo did not live in or close to WM she lived in Cooter MO. at the time. Jo did not witness Terry doing laundry she just knew it was done because during the search before my son was found the police needed something with Stevie scent on it. The only thing I had was the bandanna that I had with me during PL1 WITH Stevie scent on it. No Terry did not wash his bed linens or bedspread. Jo did not come until May 6 after Stevie was found.

Bite mark?

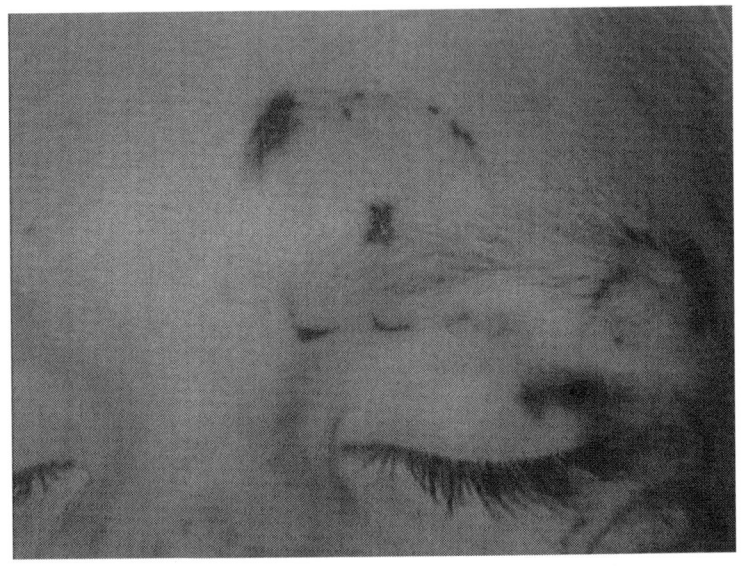

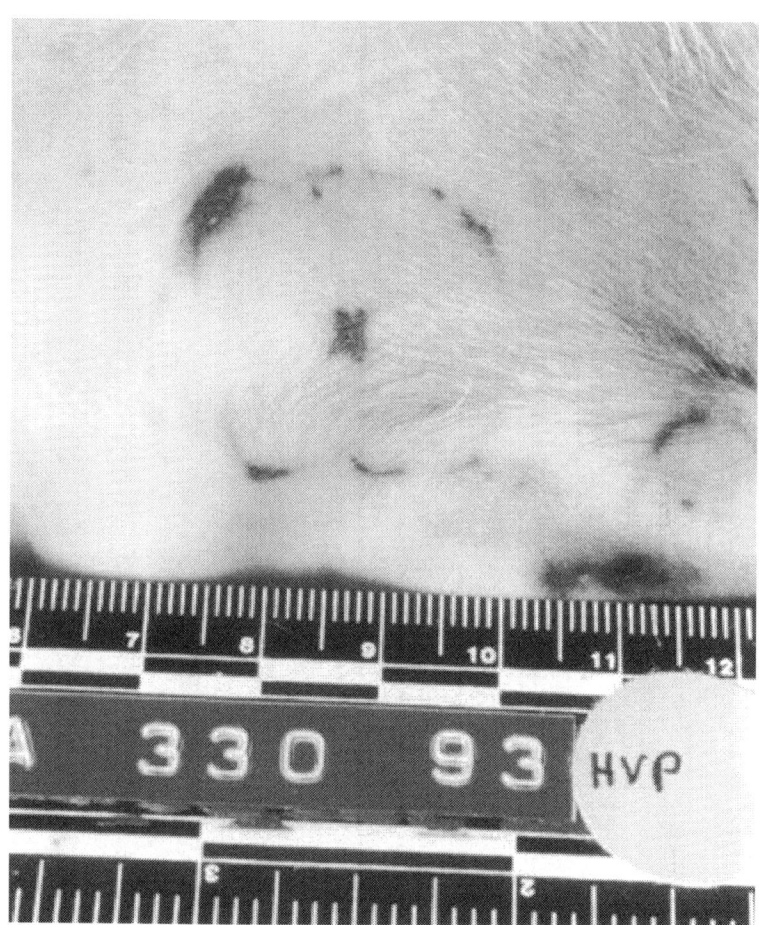

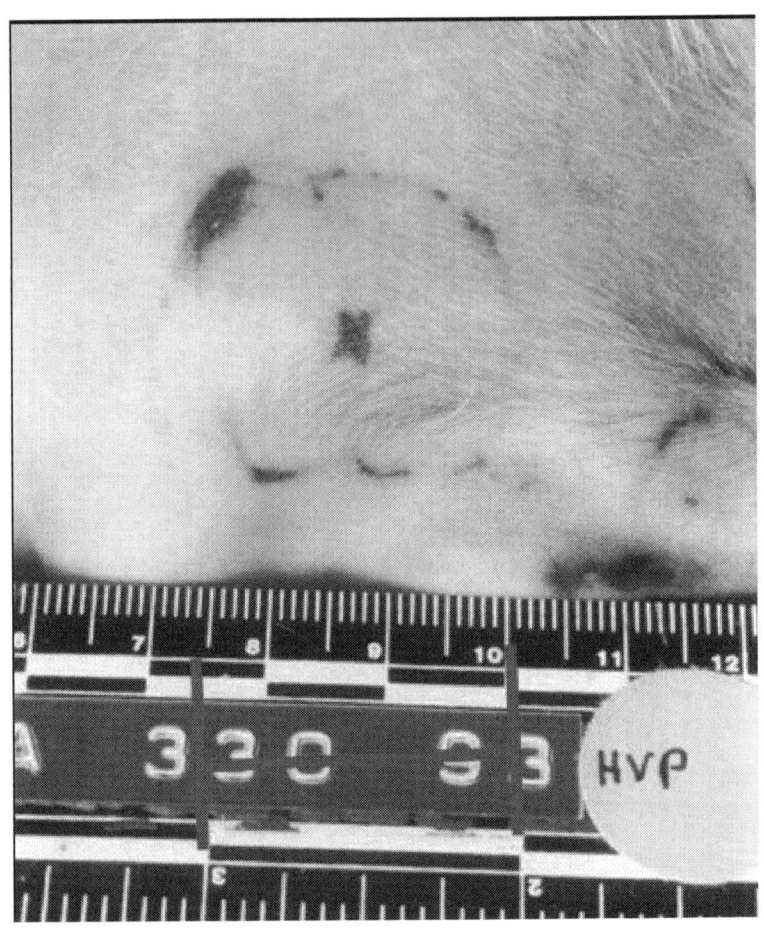

We have covered the so called bite mark pattern found on the face of Stevie Branch. We have found numerous "experts" that claim that this is in fact a bite mark made by Terry Hobbs. We had a forensic anthropologist with over 20 years' experience dealing with criminal investigations look at the wound in the picture and we asked if they felt that this could have been caused by an adult male biting the face of the child. The answer we received after a brief laugh was "Absolutely not".

The wound on the face is only 1 inch in diameter. This is noted in the autopsy photos with a ruler to measure the size of the wound. We have added an additional photo with the ruler marked to show a clear picture of the actual length of the wound at 1 inch.

The total width of this wound is exactly 1 inch as we can see the edges of the wound turning in on both sides of the wound. We then looked for something that would be an everyday item that was also 1 inch wide. We discovered that a US quarter is exactly 1 inch wide.

You can also see the "x" pattern wound found exactly dead center in the middle of the wound would match exactly to the center of the lake knife where the compass is missing.

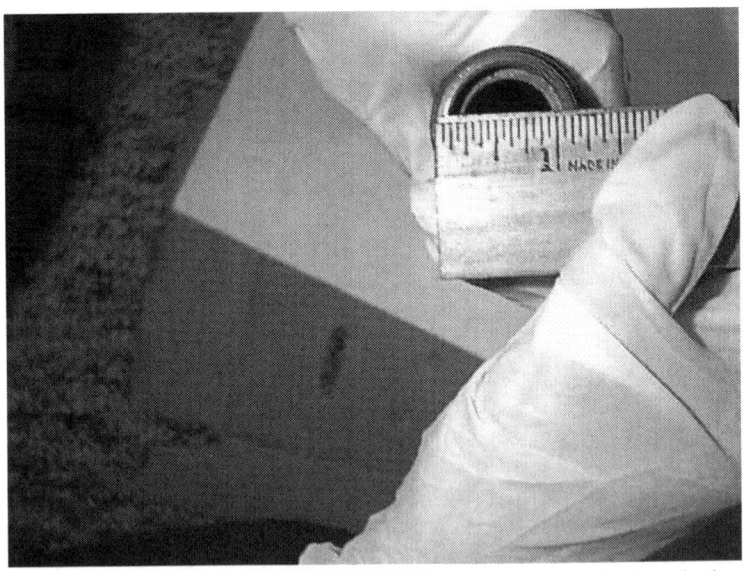

Police photo of the measurement of the lake knife

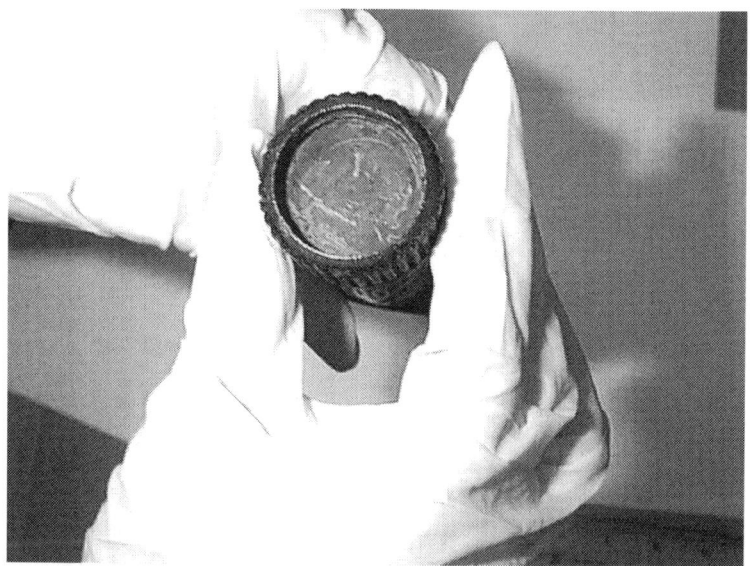

The end of the handle with the missing compass

Here is what the end of the knife would have looked like prior to the compass being broken off.

Note the pin in the middle of the compass face matches the center of the wound exactly.

Chris Morgan and Brian Holland

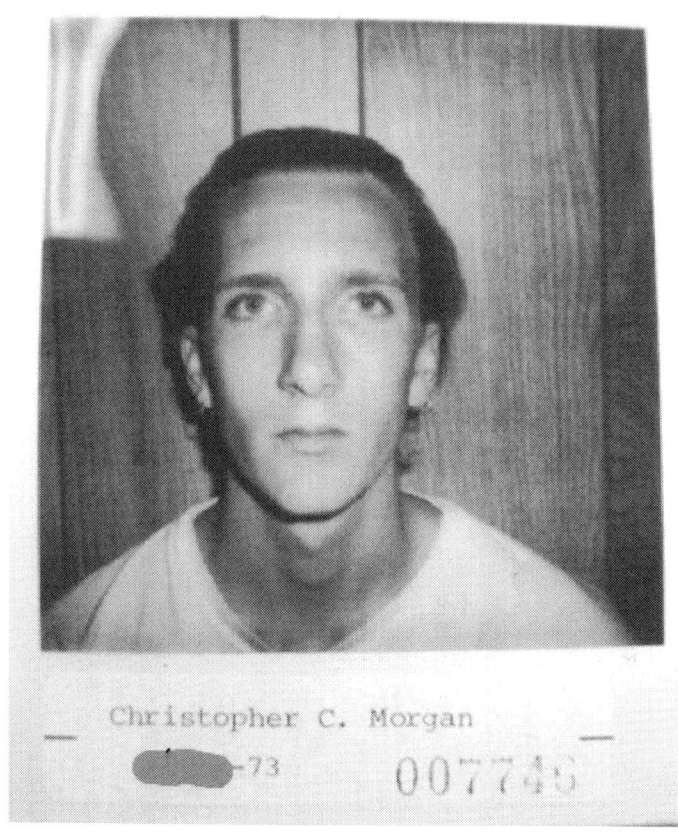

Christopher C. Morgan

Thomas Brian Holland

Chris Morgan and Brian Holland lived in West Memphis. Morgan and his parents lived on McCauley St (the same street as Steven Branch). Morgan also previously worked as an ice cream man, driving a truck selling ice cream to neighborhood children. Morgan admits to knowing Stevie Branch and his family, and he even visited the Hobbs' residence just after the murders to offer his condolences.

Just days after the murders, Morgan and Holland together left the area and went to Oceanside, California. They were questioned by police in Oceanside and each failed a polygraph test. During the interrogation in Oceanside, Morgan makes what is later described as a 'sarcastic' confession, saying that maybe be blacked out, molested, and killed the children without remembering it.

During the interview with police, Holland said he heard on the news the boys were found in a ditch. He indicated by taking his left hand to his left ankle, then his right hand to his right ankle, showing the binding positions and then changed both hands to the center of his legs demonstrating someone being tied.

Chris Morgan was also brought in to the trial for Damien and Jason. However, the jury and press were removed from the courtroom for these proceedings. Judge Burnett even went so far as to issue a gag order on this subject. Apparently, Morgan's lawyer informed the court that his client intended to invoke his Fifth Amendment right if he was required to take the stand. This of course leads to speculation that Morgan could possibly incriminate himself if forced to testify.

Could these two have killed the children or maybe even have assisted Terry Hobbs in hiding the bodies in the water later that evening? Unfortunately, we may never know the real answer to these questions or the real truth about who really committed these heinous murders.

IN CLOSING

This case has baffled the minds of many people throughout the years. Three young men convicted of capital murder with very little physical evidence tying them directly to the crime. Damien Echols, refusing to be 100% truthful about his whereabouts on the night of the murders. The eye witnesses that knew Damien and his girlfriend personally and testified that they had seen them in the area of the murders on the night of the killings.

So many unanswered questions and each one just opening the door to a new question with seemingly no answer. Why would Jessie Misskelley admit to the murders on numerous occasions when if he was in fact miles away on the day that the crimes occured?

We may never know the answers to these questions.

Will justice ever truly be served here? Or did the killers already spend 18 years of their lives in prison for a murder that they did indeed commit. As you ponder these questions in your mind, please remember who the real victims of this case are. They are really the only ones who know all the answers and they have taken them with them to their graves. They are these three beautiful young boys that were tragically taken from this world way too soon.

Michael Moore, Stevie Branch and Chris Byers

I (David) would like to thank four people who without their help, this book would never have been written:

Amanda Pettrey: Amanda brought the idea of writing this book to me and took the time out of her busy life to co-author this book with me. Without her dedication and in-depth knowledge on this case, this project would never have been started.

Jennifer Marie Lehman: Jennifer was the person who had the open mind on the facts of this case. She spent many hours looking at the evidence and crime scene photos and giving an unbiased opinion. She spent many hours online researching facts that we just did not have the time to search for. With her help, we managed to find the smallest details that may have been overlooked.

Michael Williams: Mike did all of the leg work on the ground, he spent days on end interviewing witnesses and traveling to Arkansas to investigate this story for us.

Mike is a former homicide investigator so his knowledge of murder scenes and homicide investigations was a great asset to this book. We spent many late nights and early mornings on the phone trying to piece this whole puzzle together. Even though I feel that there are still a lot of pieces missing to this puzzle.

And I want to say a special thank you to the person who helped me deal with the mental part of writing this book.

Tabatha Wilburn: The hardest part of this book was dealing with the emotions that go through you when you have to view crime scene photos of little kids. Too many nights I went to bed with these images burned into my memory and falling asleep was not an option for me. When I came to the point where I felt that I just could not do this anymore and really considered ending the whole project, she held me in her arms and kissed me and made me realize that life is not all crime scene photos and autopsy reports. Without her I would have given up on writing this book all together.

I (Amanda), would like to offer my sincerest thanks to a few people that have helped me so much through the process of helping to co-author my first book.

David Pietras: I have read several of Dave's books and one day I just took a chance and friend requested him on Facebook and sent him a message telling him how much I had enjoyed reading one of his recent true crime stories. Who knew that would turn into the two of us writing a book together? He has listened to my passion for this story and opened the door for me to be able to contribute to the telling of this story. I appreciate all that he has done for me and all the work that he has invested into this book. He has invested time, money and so much more into this work and I am humbled to have my name next to his on the cover.

Mike Williams: Even though I have never met him face to face, this book wouldn't be possible if it weren't for Mike and all the work that he did for us so that we could find all the facts of this case. Mike has went through more than any one person should ever have to while this writing has been taking place, and yet he never stopped, never gave up and never gave in. I appreciate his dedication and his help more than he will ever know.

My mom, Judy Meadows: She has supported me from day one on this project and has encouraged me and been there for me in any way that I needed her to be. She is my best friend and I am so thankful that I have been able to share this experience with her.

My children: They are the light of my life and the reason that I live. They have given up a lot of "mommy time" so that I could work on this book, but they have done it without complaint and have been so supportive and understanding. I love them more than words can ever say.

Last, but certainly not least, I want to say a special thank you to my partner in life, my husband: ,

Greg: Greg is my anchor, my rock, and the love of my life. I couldn't do anything if it weren't for him. He has supported me through this process, cheered me on, given me advice, read and watched things pertaining to this case with me, loved me and helped me in any way that I needed him. I am the luckiest woman on earth to be married to such a great man. Saying thank you to him is not nearly enough, but I do thank him because he deserves that and so much more.

Printed in Great Britain
by Amazon